Wake up!

There's only one way to get
out of that rut you are in...

Leanne Magoulias
Written with Kelly Hender

Copyright © 2017

All rights reserved. This book or any portion thereof may not be reproduced or used in any manner whatsoever without the express written permission of the author except for the use of brief quotations in a book review.

Client names have been changed to protect the privacy of individuals.

Printed in Australia First Printing, 2017
ISBN: 978-0-6480806-5-7

Cover design by Aaron Cliff

This book would not be possible without my clients. Thank you for your trust, for taking the hard road with me and for your continued support.

Contents

Introduction:	**1**
Chapter 1: How I was woken up	**5**
Chapter 2: How do you get stuck in a rut?	**39**
Chapter 3: It's time to wake up	**65**
Chapter 4: Confront your emotions and you will master life	**99**
Chapter 5: All of your relationships are a reflection of you	**127**
Chapter 6: The evolution of you	**149**
Appendix A	**185**
Acknowledgements	**187**
About the author	**190**

Introduction

In any given situation, at any given time, in your life you are given two very clear and distinct choices—one is easy and the gain is immediate, the other is harder with a not-so obvious gain. Which of those two choices do you tend to make? I already know your answer, I base it on the sheer number of people who seek out my help every day because a wrong choice led to more wrong choices and they got stuck in a rut.

I'm a medium and I work in Sydney. I'm not the fluffy kind of medium who tells you about your dead grandpa Joe and how much he loved you, nor am I the kind who tells you I can see riches around the corner. I'm the hard-knocks medium who will call you on your bullshit because I can see your soul fighting against the desires of your human body, which are blocking you from facing up to your reality. If you don't like being told how it is, don't read on. I'm not trying to sell you more books. I'm on a mission to help humanity and I say it like it is because it needs to be said. If you don't fix your life right now, in this life, you will repeat your life over and over again until you learn to fix it.

Have you ever had deja vu where you felt as if

you've had the same experience or been in the same place before, but you just can't quite catch the how or why? It's just a fleeting memory but when you try to trace it back in this life it escapes you. You have been here before; your soul carries the memory of it and that's where that deja vu feeling comes from. It has been estimated that the main character, Phil, In the movie *Groundhog Day*, gets stuck in a time loop of repeating the same day over and over for decades, or possibly even longer, before he realises the lesson and gets himself out of it. I see every member of humanity stuck in a similar time loop, living and repeating our mistakes until we die. Worse still, you will repeat it all over again in the next life, and the next, and the next until you get it right.

Did you think you were going to get away with your crimes against another human? It doesn't work like that. You kill a person in this life, you get to experience being killed in the next life—and that is the true meaning of karma. You sell drugs in this life, which people die from, you take that karma onto the next life and live the life of a drug addict. You cheat on your partner in this life, you get to experience the pain of living with a cheating partner in the next life. It's simple; if you inflict pain on another human being in this life, you get to live in their shoes in the next life with that pain inflicted on you. Committing suicide isn't really an option because no matter what, you're coming back to do it all over, again and again, until you learn. Just like Phil.

So, here are your two choices in this situation: take the easy road, put this book down and continue giving into all of life's temptations; affairs, drugs, booze, dirty money and pay the price of it in the next life—or carry on reading, take the harder road with me and fix your problems now.

Chapter 1
How I was woken up

When a client walks through my clinic door, I ask them to fill out a questionnaire. As they concentrate on the task of writing, I step into their body to see what their life is like from their point of view. I do this to get a general reading before a client can tell me their specific problem. Often a client will get nervous about the telling, so the questionnaire keeps them busy and their body neutral so I can become them, uninterrupted by their nerves. A client came through my door a few years ago and as I became her—Annie is her name—I could feel her life just as if I was her: I could feel that Annie's marriage, home life and children's fighting were all causing her a lot of stress and she was barely coping. If I was to articulate Annie's thoughts or internal monologue, it sounds something like this:

Annie: Every day for as long as I can remember I have felt trapped, isolated, lonely, depressed, worthless, and suicidal. I'm often told I'm worthless, as if I'm like a scum on the sole of someone's shoe that they can't get off. It hurts to breathe as I hear; "you're disgusting", "retard", "you're pathetic", "what would an idiot like you know?" These words and worse come from my husband's mouth. The same mouth that whispered, "I love you" once upon a time. We had a good start: he was really charming and sexy. I fell for him pretty hard, almost instantly. It was like an amazing whirlwind of love and we married within a year and our first baby followed shortly after. Within a few years, we were a family with two kids. I can't pinpoint when it turned sour, he just had a few moods every so often. I didn't like it but I tried to keep the peace as best I could. Everyone says forgiveness is important in a marriage—I wanted to do the right thing, so I forgave him for the sake of our kids and our families. In those early days, he would get over it and he would cuddle me and make me laugh so I forgave quite easily. After each mood I kind of forget it happened, I just got on with the kids and my life. The gaps between the moods became less and less. It's hard to know when they're going to strike him now, they kind of catch you unaware.

Like the other night, a question about my day turned into a verbal bashing about me leaving the bathroom unclean because I had mentioned having lunch with my sister between running household errands. When this happens, I just keep my head down and get busy doing my chores. A few times his words have made me so angry that I have lost control and told him to shut up and that he's not God or my father, but it just made it worse—his face was full of pure rage and hate when his fist connected with my cheek. He was really sorry after, he told me he didn't mean it that he loved me and he hadn't meant to hurt me. I know I shouldn't have provoked him, he was so devastated that he had hurt me. It doesn't sound right but I felt so close to him after that, he was gentle and caring when all of his anger had gone... I forgave him for everyone's sake. The moodiness is not his fault, he says, he just gets really angry. But the trauma of the beating doesn't go away, you can't just can't kiss a punch away from your memory.

    The kids help calm the tension between us, he's so good with them. I love watching them together because my husband is like a soft, gentle loving person when he's with his children. He will do anything for them, I really can't fault him there. He is a great father. My son is starting to show similar moods, I don't know if he is just copying his idol but he takes it out on my daughter. I don't like it when he attacks her; it makes me so angry. My son doesn't behave this way when his father is around. Nor is my husband moody or critical towards me in front of others, in fact no-one would be able to tell that we are in conflict. He acts quite loving, I think he likes to put it on for others. Social occasions are both the best and the worst of times. Whiles he's very loving towards me in front of everyone, afterwards he gets extremely moody. All sorts of accusations get flung, "You're an embarrassment!" "You just want to be the centre of attention!" I try explaining the situation but he keeps telling me how I was behaving and my thoughts get all confused, I worry about it, *had I wanted the attention like he said? Did I talk a bit too long to the waiter to explain how I liked my meal... did I smile too much at the man across the table?*

*****

When Annie finished with the form we discussed her reasons for seeing me. Annie's mother had rung to say she had overheard one of Stan's tirades— explaining how Annie had failed to hang up properly on their call the night before and she had heard everything. She told Annie she had suspected things weren't right for a while and after hearing Stan's verbal attack she was so concerned she wanted to call the authorities and report him. Annie didn't think Stan's anger was as bad as her mother made out, but she did admit she numbed herself to hearing the worst of it so she wasn't sure how bad it had actually sounded over the phone.

I told Annie that her body has the memory, even if she wasn't consciously aware of it at the time. To demonstrate this, I asked her to lie down on my massage table. I covered her eyes with a mask. I guided her to come into her heart by thinking of the love she has for her children. As I felt this love overwhelm her, I asked her to stay in that place and not return into her head or thoughts. *'Focus on the feeling in your heart, and how much you love your children. From here, in your heart, go back to 5 minutes before Stan came home when you were talking to your mother.'* The love Annie has for her children grounded her body into a contented place. *'Now go to when Stan arrived home.'* Immediately stress overwhelmed Annie's body. *'Can you feel the difference in those situations in your body?'* Annie nodded. As we continued and I asked her if she had ever witnessed this kind of conflict in her parents' marriage, I already knew the answer—I could read it in her DNA. Annie's verbal answer to me was no, she hadn't witnessed conflict between her parents in her childhood home. This is true, but as I went further back into her ancestry to her grandparents' marriage, I found the vibration of abuse there in Annie's DNA. This emotional inheritance was passed to Annie's mother and through her to Annie.

We inherit an emotional blueprint from our parents, just as they inherited from their parents. This emotional inheritance can be passed through seven generations. These ancestral emotions are not always activated, which is why Annie's mother had a peaceful marriage. Annie's grandmother lived with conflict in her marriage in Serbia and I could feel her fear that her husband would actually fulfil his threats to throw her out of the home—being the 1950s, when women had to rely on their husbands for financial support, she would have been destitute—so she copped the abuse, keeping her head down and her mouth shut. Just like Annie.

I went another generation further back but there was no abuse there. I came back into Annie's mother to see how this dysfunction had skipped a generation.

Annie's mother had grown up in Serbia witnessing her mother being belittled and verbally abused by her father, I could feel her strength and determination that she would not experience the same in her marriage. She had made the choice that she wouldn't marry a man like her father, so she actively sought out a peaceful partner and at any sign of abuse or the start of a pattern of abuse, she stood up to it and set the boundary to prevent it occurring. Annie had grown up in a home with a loving family, so the fact that she had attracted the same situation as her grandmother confirmed the inheritance of the dysfunctional emotion in the DNA.

Annie's emotional vibration was familiar to me— I had a similar abuse trait in my family's DNA. I grew up witnessing my father verbally abuse my mother, and at times he would direct his verbal abuse and fists on my four siblings and I. Dad had various health problems, which meant he couldn't always support his family and that led to him taking his frustration and anger out on everyone around him. **When I realised my DNA had the answers to my life's problems, I knew I could use this emotional inheritance theory to help a lot of people.** But developing my ability to heal myself, as well as others didn't happen overnight...

My Story

As a child I was, and still am of course, extremely sensitive to other people's emotional pain and sadness. If Dad hit my siblings, I could feel both his anger and frustration as well as my sibling's pain and hurt. I didn't know at the time that the emotions were not my own, it just seemed as if worry and fear were constantly in my thoughts. Imagine being pulled in different directions; feeling worry one moment, then incredible sadness the next without knowing the cause of the emotion. Plus, I was a child so I wouldn't have been able to articulate the emotions I was feeling, I just worried about everything. All the time. Picking up the anger, misery and sadness from members of my family often led to my childhood mind imagining them all getting sick and dying. I could also feel their joy, but the fear and worry were overpowering. The tension and conflict in my home took a toll on me and I became highly strung. The only relief from the emotional roller-coaster was to find a way to escape it.

Hiding under my bed became a habit when I heard Dad raise his voice in anger. Under my bed, it was calm... I would lie and imagine myself travelling away from my room, out of the house full of emotional pain and float into the universe. I didn't have a name for it, but I now know it to be astro travel through dimensions. I would meet people there who would embrace me and fill me with their love, warmth and wisdom. My child's mind didn't know these were spirits and that I was in another world—to me it was an amazing comfort, as if my body had become weightless, floating in a big, fluffy cloud. Every emotional pain and ache in my body was gone and I felt light. I was continuously drawn back to this place of lightness, love and comfort as a soothing balm to the pain and discomfort of my everyday life.

My Ability

Escaping my mediocre life became a habit of mine. If I went with Mum to help clean the retirement homes I would listen, fascinated, to the stories of the elderly residents. She could leave me with them for hours, and I would be enthralled by their stories. I wanted so much to feel what it was like to live through their life, and as I listened to them it would feel as if I was living their life for those brief hours. As time went on, I became aware that I wasn't just getting caught up in their stories; I genuinely felt them, as if I was in their body, living their life. I didn't realise I was adding to their stories with the details I was reading from their lives, of family members that had passed on, until I noticed they all seemed to ask, "How do you know that?" a fair bit. I never questioned where this information came from, I was just open to the experience of living in their world to escape mine and in seconds I would know what it was like to live their life and I knew everything about them.

Becoming a person as if I'm in their body and living their life is only one element of my ability, I can also communicate with spirits. As a child, when I didn't know how to filter them out, they would visit me while I was sleeping. The fright I would get from these visits added to the huge burden of worry and fear weighing on me. Some visits had me screaming the house awake in the middle of the night. My parents never seemed phased—spirits and Mediums are common in Greek culture, and the ability is evident in my family history—they just seemed to accept it. My siblings were scared by the night terrors and would refuse to let me sleep next to them. I couldn't sleep alone, so I would fake sleep until I could feel their body and know they were in a deep enough sleep that it was safe to climb into their bed. They couldn't work out how I got there, but they became used to finding me in their bed in the mornings. Of course, my brothers had fun tormenting my fears with their pranks, hanging dolls or items in doorways to scare me into thinking it was a spirit. I was highly strung; so it worked more often than not, I hate to admit!

    But as a teenager it was the visits to the retirement homes that brought my attention to my 'ability' as something beyond seeing spirits at night. I began to recognise some of the rooms had a different feeling, as if they were cooler than others. I describe it as a cold feeling, but in energy terms it's like an open window, as if a portal leading to another dimension was in the room. Some rooms would be cold, while others were warm. Over time and exposure, I realised the change to the room came from the energy of the person living in it. The coldness meant the elderly resident was near death. I didn't know anything about that person and I wouldn't always enquire or bother them, I just cleaned, but often we would return the next week and the cold room would be empty and that person had passed on.

Talking to God

As my awareness of my ability became stronger, so did my fears rise with the different feelings and images I was getting from spirits. I attended my Greek Orthodox church and prayed to God for guidance. This brought me a sense of peace, so I continued praying at night by my bed. I began to realise the peace came from connecting with my heart to talk to God. And he was sending messages back. They were like a whisper at first, but as my awareness grew, so did the messages. (Read Neale Donald Walsch's book *Conversations with God*—it's as he describes.) I can only liken it to the same voice inside you that tells you right from wrong. It's quiet, almost unnoticeable, so it's easy to understand why so many people don't focus on it and either miss it or cover it with their everyday thoughts and concerns. I became aware of it because I had so many questions about life and the universe. I suddenly started finding the answers within my own self. When this happened, it felt like the void in my chest was filled with an unconditional love and I would *know* the answer. I can't describe this other than knowing there was more than just this world and our existence. **Knowing the answer was in this connection in my heart, not in my head.**

Medium

A visit to the cemetery in my teens gave me a different understanding about the extent of my ability to communicate with spirits. At 13, and in a bid to avoid the school sheriff scouting the hot spots for truants, I skipped school with some neighbourhood girls to hang out in the cemetery. If you'd asked me about cemeteries, I would likely have rattled off something about peaceful souls resting as I'd learnt in my Greek Orthodox studies. I was to learn a very different lesson that day.

We entered around 11am and from the moment I stepped through the gate, it was like entering another world. I can only describe it as an out-of-body experience. I didn't talk to the other girls, I just roamed the cemetery as if the graves were calling to me. Every grave told a story of the deceased person and their families; there was a heaviness of grief at each one. It was as if I had actually been there when they lowered the person into the ground. I knew information about the life of the person in the grave and how that life had ended.

Grave after grave told a similar story of grief; my whole body was swamped with the amount of sadness. The graves that were quiet seemed eerie in contrast, and I knew those people had died with no family around them. The strength of the emotions frightened me, but I also felt numbed as if I was in a trance. **I knew then that not only could I read spirits but also the people in their lives that were connected to them.**

After a while, my friends and I dozed off under a tree. We woke at 3pm and left the cemetery. It wasn't until we were well away from it that we came out of the numbness and wondered what had actually happened. It's as if we'd visited a different dimension in the hours we had spent there. One of the girls explained her experience as feeling tormented by demons, while the other experienced an empty place—a nothingness. We went our separate ways that afternoon and never saw each other again. Many years later I heard one of the girls had taken her own life and the other became a drug addict. I feel lucky to be the only one of the three with my life intact. I often wondered whether this was a coincidence, or did something that day change the girls and lead them down a darker path...

Seeing the past

I left school when I was 16 to work with my sister in a nursing home. I was keen to help people and I was also besotted with the elderly residents. Instead of going to lunch I would sit with them, learning about their lives. I would tell them what I knew about their lives and either they would ask, 'how did you know?' or they would accept the information. Some would even tell me they believed I was psychic. It was like a form of confession for them; they would tell me things they had never told others. I could see their parents or grandparents and the life they had lived as children, as well as the life they had lived with their own children. I could simply see beyond their stories, as only a person living their own life would know. The best way I can describe how I can see or read someone's life is how you would recall a dream after waking, where you can still feel the emotions of the dream. That's how I pick up an event that's happened in someone's life—but it feels as if I am one with them. At first it was difficult to know if the information I picked up was them telling me or I was reading it. The conversations were almost telepathic, in that I couldn't distinguish them from my thoughts. I didn't consciously recognise them as a 'reading'.

Negative effects

Within a year of working in the nursing home, I began to feel a heavy emotional burden, like depression. In hindsight, and with many years of experience working with people's emotions, I know I was collecting the pain of the elderly residents. I began to avoid the afternoon shifts—that's usually when family life kicks in after work and I think the residents felt lonely without that family routine that had been part of their lives for so many years.

By 21, I was working as a community nurse doing home care with quadriplegics. I spent weeknights soccer training, and Saturdays playing games. During one game, I landed head first into the ground and heard an internal cracking sound underneath my ear. I got up, disorientated, and a rush of pain down my spine nearly had me falling back to the ground. Luckily, I was caught by a teammate who helped me to a bench. Coach quickly took me to the hospital where an X-ray showed I had damaged my vertebrae. I was put in a neck brace and advised to go home and come back in six weeks for a check-up. Every fear and worry I'd had in my life up to this point doesn't describe the fear and anxiety that took over my thoughts. I was paralysed with worry. *Would I become a quadriplegic? I can't live like that!* I was desperate not to have to go through the pain and suffering I'd seen my patients deal with.

At the following check-up, they removed the brace and assessed the damage. Aside from noting a little stiffness, they sent me home to come back in another six weeks for a check-up. When I returned, I complained of pins and needles, but was advised I would be fine. I panicked that the pins and needles would lead to numbness and then paralysis. I found my thoughts going into a downward spiral of anxiety, panic and fear. It was a dark, scary place. I couldn't eat, sleep or focus on anything else without getting dragged back to the *'what ifs'* that went round and round my head.

At my next visit, my doctor said he believed the symptoms I described were mental not physical and antidepressants could help me with the emotional battle. Despite my paralysing fear, I thought it would be better to fight the depression as naturally as I could without medication (I'm not recommending this, it just felt like it was the best decision for me at the time). I already had some interest in alternative ideas, so I explored meditation and other relaxation methods for an alternative way of dealing with my emotional battle. It was the first time in my life I attempted to connect to spirituality outside of religion.

This went on for two years and I learnt many things about combating fear and depression, but I also came to understand how to listen to my body. I knew something was wrong with my neck and that it wasn't my mental state. I fought for and got an appointment with a neurologist, who after assessing me, insisted on operating immediately. He booked me in for an operation the next day. While I was relieved to finally have a diagnosis, my fears were bigger than ever. *What if something went wrong during the operation!* Having witnessed first-hand the hardships quadriplegics faced, I knew this was something I didn't want to experience. I prayed, *'God, I give you my soul. If I'm meant to die, let me die, but don't let me be a quadriplegic. If I'm meant to live, use me as a tool. If I'm meant to help all these people, I devote my life to that.'*

The next morning, I had a six-hour operation. My surgeon came to see me shortly after and at this stage, I'd forgotten all about my promise. His first words were, jokingly, 'Whoever you prayed to, you owe big. Your vertebrae C5 and C6 were disintegrated. I don't even know how your neck was holding your head up. So whoever you prayed to, you owe BIG TIME!'

I healed from the operation quickly and six weeks later, returned to light duties at work. I was rostered to visit senior citizens in their homes. I noticed, more than usual, people (sometimes complete strangers) were seeking me out and during our conversations I could guide them to the right solution. I don't say this with ego, I just noticed that when they shared their problem, I had access to the answer within me and could give them the direction they needed.

Awakening

One of the retirement villages I was asked to visit had a weekly art class and I got excited about getting stuck into something creative to take my mind off my rehabilitation. I asked the art teacher if I could learn to paint with the senior citizens on my day off. We agreed I could sit in and help him while I learnt. After a few weeks, Eileen, a resident in my art class I'd grown friendly with, asked me to visit her at home. I gave her the aged-care administration details and forgot all about it. I didn't even register it was her when I got her name and address for my house call the following week. When Eileen greeted me at her door she said, 'I specifically asked for you.' I didn't find this unusual; I'd become accustomed to people saying this to me. But Eileen didn't seem like she needed the help or attention. Assuming she was lonely, I sat with her every day for the rest of the week and we talked about her life.

I returned the second week to chat as usual, when Eileen asked mid-conversation, 'Do you see and hear things other people can't?'
Before I could respond, she added, 'What's your belief?'

I told her I was Greek Orthodox, but as I admitted it I also became worried. *Was she questioning me because she was a devil worshipper or involved in a cult?*

But she didn't talk about religion, she said, 'I'm going to tell you something. Do you believe in past lives?'

'I'm open to it,' I replied.

'Do you believe we are chosen to come onto this Earth?'

'No, not really.'

'You've got a purple aura all around you,' she said. I didn't know what an aura was, and she explained it was an energy field. Then she pulled out books from under her bed. At a glance, the titles seemed to be about spirituality, pyramids, ruins, Egyptian history and the like.

'I'm going to tell you something. I don't want to scare you,' she said. 'I've been waiting for you for a long time. I finally see it. You asked me in the last life to awaken you. You were a master of spirituality and you asked me to awaken you in this life.'

I didn't understand what she meant and I felt a bit spooked. We carried on talking about other things.

But as I was leaving, she said, 'Within a week, you'll awaken and understand everything I've said today.'

I smiled and nodded, while thinking, *she's lost it. She's not well, and I need to get the hell out of this place because she's mad.*

But it happened just like she said. Within a week, I woke up one day and I suddenly had the answers to all my questions about the universe and human existence. The questions that had caused a feeling of emptiness my whole life were suddenly answered. Since I was eight years old, I had been asking questions like, *'What is the purpose for my existence on this earth? Why am I Leanne? Why did I come here? Why did I pick this family?'* Suddenly I knew the answers. I could feel, like I did that day in the cemetery, a connection to the universe. I felt my soul was open and the answers were within it. I could see clearly how the human body dysfunction affected the soul's journey in each life and caused the soul to live more lives to fulfil its purpose. I could also see, from a bird's-eye view, how every member of humanity was fighting against the other's self-importance. I could see how each soul was truly fighting for peace and love, but the 'selfishness' of each human character was ultimately winning the battle. I could see how everyone was a 'legend' in their own thoughts and this contributed to the selfishness and separation of humanity.

With my new awareness, I began connecting with others in the spiritual community. **It felt like oneness with a real community—something I hadn't felt a belonging to before.** The people I met and the information I discovered fulfilled a part of me that had been missing. Soon enough, more and more people heard about my ability and sought me out for readings.

Readings

My readings started off as psychometric, where I held a piece of my client's jewellery. Like the questionnaire sheet I now use, holding a client's item helped them focus away from their own thoughts and it reduced their nerves so I could read their body uninterrupted. I noticed that as I let go of my fears around spirits, my ability to read people strengthened.

In one particular reading; I learnt the dark side of the spirit world. A friend in the spiritual community asked me to do a reading for her visitor, Jack, who was from the US. My first impression of Jack was that he looked like he'd walked out of an American TV show in his oversized jeans and T-shirt. I put his age at about 28. He didn't share any details of his life with me, but as I held his sports watch, feeling the warmth from his body still on it, I looked back into his life. I knew he had a girlfriend and I told him he would have a good life in Australia.

As I was looking at him and feeling his energy, I connected with his soul. This connection allows me to wind back to the earlier years of someone's life rather than read the here-and-now of their current life. Suddenly, I was him and he was 14 years old selling drugs on the streets in a city that was foreign to my current life, but that I knew was in the US, — somewhere like New Orleans. I saw a person approach him and exchange words. He took the cash that was offered in one hand, while his other hand extended a packet full of a white powder that I knew to be illegal drugs. I saw this scene more than once and I knew he had been a drug dealer.

I can connect with another person through the person I'm reading, so I could see some of the people who had bought Jack's drugs had overdosed and died. As I came back to Jack's body, I could feel all the spirits around him that had died from the drugs he had sold them. Without his knowledge, he carried the bad energy, like karma, because he was the one who gave them a substance that caused their death. I told him what I saw and he confirmed that he came to Australia to get away from his old life. He felt he had a second chance and he was going to create a new life here.

As I left, I realised I was trembling and I felt overly anxious. That night I slept fitfully and dreamt strange, dark and morbid things, as if the spirits around Jack were showing me their hell. I woke up in a bad way and couldn't shake the anxious feelings that had come to me in my dreams.

Fighting my fears

As the day progressed, the feelings got worse and I began to worry that the fear and anxiety were taking a hold of me. I sought out Michael, my spiritual adviser, for guidance. He explained that I was leaving myself open in the readings and the spirits around Jack had attached to me and were passing on their fears of dying. They thought I could help them cross over.

'Spirits can't trigger these emotions, unless you have them in you,' he explained. Michael's solution was to clear my energy using reiki. I felt the anxiety leave but then it just boomeranged straight back onto me. I started crying. 'Leanne, you've got to be stronger than that,' Michael said. 'Fight it.' So, I visualised armour around my body like a shield and I yelled, 'I'm not going to accept this.' I felt my fears leave.

As soon as I went home they came back again. I felt weak, upset and confused about what to do. I knew I was going through this for a reason, but I was also desperate to find relief. That night, weak from all the emotions, I prayed to God to ask for help. *'Get me out of this again, I know my purpose now,'* I said. *'Teach me how to get out of this and I promise to help thousands of people who go through anxiety and fear.'* Then I let some of the anxiety go, having faith I would be guided to find the way out.

I took a shower to cleanse myself and as soon as I stepped under the water, a white light came into the room. I could feel it wrapping around me from the tip of my toes, up around my body like armour. I felt the strength of my soul and the white light protecting me. Finally I felt strong, as if I was an armoured soldier; I was a 'soul-dier'. I knew from that moment on my purpose would be fulfilled.

God's voice came into my awareness and I heard, *'You're on a journey now. You start your journey from here onwards.'* I felt incredible strength come over me. I knew I was to be a teacher and that I would spend my life fighting my fear and anxiety, and that this would take me on a path to find techniques that I could pass on to others.

For the next few years, I explored healing techniques while I continued my readings. I also studied body-work therapy. It wasn't easy to gain my qualifications with my dyslexia, but I knew I had been given a learning difficulty so that I could inspire others and empathise with their pain. My clients reported that my massage work not only lifted physical aches and pains but also their emotional burdens too. As I gained more experience with therapy, I began reading terminal illnesses in the body and could advise people to seek medical help. I could also work with disabilities in the body to give people relief. As time went on, I learnt to fine-tune my ability to help as many people as I could. As I helped one client, they would send me more as news of my healing abilities spread.

Relationship reflections

By the time I was 27, I knew it was time to enter into the next stage of life to experience my lessons with my own family. It's through family life with my husband Sam and our children Stephen and Peter that I have received more insights on the emotional DNA inheritance theory. As I watched my children grow and react to the world, I saw very clearly my own inherited dysfunctions and those of my husband's in them and the effect it had on their behaviour. I realised I couldn't blame my parents, or my ancestors before them, when my husband and I had passed on our dysfunctions in the same way. This understanding also removed the blame I put on myself, and instead I vowed to use my ability and insights to help other people; to become aware of their inherited emotional DNA so that they could prevent them from passing onto their children.

I spent years investigating my own emotional inheritance through my family life with Sam and the kids, and as my own emotions came up, I asked for guidance to heal them. Healing my dysfunctions also benefited my children, as I used the tactics I was learning to convince their subconscious to push out the emotion. As this occurred in my personal life, my client work naturally evolved where I could help people unhook the emotions they had inherited through their DNA. They marvelled after each healing session how situations that had previously bothered them now no longer did. Overtime and many sessions, my clients' feedback confirmed my guidance on healing their emotional dysfunctions was working: the consensus among them was that their previous reactions, which they had struggled to control, were replaced with a wisdom or 'a knowing' what do in any situation—it was as if they had found an emotional maturity that brought peace into their lives.

Let's return to Annie's experience; where we had found the inheritance of abuse in her DNA that had been created in her grandmother and was passed on to her mother and then into Annie. This inheritance played out when Annie met Stan—they both had the same abuse trait in their DNA that would have identified as a match to them when they met. Have you ever travelled overseas and spotted someone in the distance and recognised a familiarity? You scan their face to work out how you might know them. Through a quick process of elimination, you know that you haven't actually met them before but the familiarity they carry is because they are Greek (or whatever nationality you are). You just know, without even having to ask them. When two people come together with a similar trait—like Annie and Stan's abusive trait—**the emotional inheritance creates a strong sense of familiarity** like this that makes them feel a connection, as if they have known each other a long time.

Since Annie had numbed her response to Stan's verbal attacks because they were too difficult to listen to, I needed to show her that her body has a memory and it had used the numbing as a defence mechanism—a form of self-protection. From this memory, I guided Annie with a visualisation technique to the source in her DNA. As Annie lay on the massage table and I became her, I could guide her with words to visualise her mother standing in front of her and all of her mother's ancestors on both sides behind her standing one after the other as far as her third eye (see appendix A) could take her. Then I asked her to look down and see an umbilical cord between her and her mother, linking them together. From there we visualised Annie using a tool to release the inherited emotion from her body—some clients visualise a super-powered hose blasting the emotion out, others use a pick to hack at it... whatever works for the individual client at the time.

As Annie attacked the abusive inheritance with an axe, I asked her to come behind the emotion and state clearly and loudly with her heart's voice to her mother that; 'I will not inherit, nor will I take on any emotion to do with... abuse.' When I felt the emotion was gone from her body, I asked her to visualise it going through the umbilical cord back to her mother and ancestors. When that was done, Annie visualised herself cutting the cord and her ancestors floating into space, taking the emotion with it. **This visualisation tool is very effective in tricking the subconscious into believing the emotion is gone.**

Over the subsequent weeks, Annie returned and along with the visualisation healings, we spent time talking each week about her home life and I advised her how to play out the situations she was encountering. As time went on Annie found her strength—the same strength her mother had used to break the abusive pattern. After a while, it became apparent that Stan wouldn't change his behaviour and Annie's new strength wouldn't allow her to take the verbal abuse. Plus Stan was showing signs of his anger escalating and Annie began to worry that his anger would turn to physical violence. Her children's safety and her own were at risk.

Eventually with her new strength and wisdom, Annie decided enough was enough, so she sought the assistance she needed to take her children and leave Stan. He reacted with shock—he had never thought there was a consequence to his behaviour because he had never experienced one before in his relationship. Stan's world was upended and he was forced to confront his actions. He tried very hard to convince Annie to come home but she resisted. After a lengthy break she gave him a glimmer of hope, she told him that they would start over again as if they had just met. He was allowed to ask her on a date. She told him she would see how that went and if it went well and he asked her again, she would go on another date and they would continue in this way like a courtship. This didn't sit well with Stan at first, but he soon realised Annie was standing firm and it was the only avenue to get his family back. Just like any new relationship should start, at any sign of bad behaviour from Stan, Annie firmly stood up to it. One incident resulted in Stan losing control of his anger and pushing Annie. While she recognised similarities to their earlier courtship days, Annie realised where she had gone wrong and firmly issued Stan with an ultimatum: "get help with your anger or you won't see your children again" she told him. The Anger management courses Stan enlisted in helped him learn the tools for managing his anger. Eventually over a period of time, Stan proved himself and Annie agreed to return.

There is no such thing as happily ever after—relationships require work and both Annie and Stan had to do their own work to keep from slipping back into bad habits. Annie had to continue to maintain her boundaries at the sign of Stan losing control of his anger, and Stan had to fight falling into a complacency and keep on top of his anger management for the good of his family life. Years later, they have come to a peaceful place in their relationship and they are continuing to work hard to maintain that peace.

Take the time to consider all the relationships in your life—the purpose of any relationship—from co-worker to life partner—is to reflect your own traits. If you are reacting negatively to your partner or anyone else in your life, it's an indication of a dysfunction in you. I firmly believe **those who bring out the worst in us are in fact our greatest teachers because they highlight our emotional dysfunctions** and once we know what they are, we can heal them.

Chapter 2
How did you get stuck in a rut?

Underneath the common everyday thoughts that your conscious mind focuses on—*where did I leave the car keys... I must remember to pick up milk on the way home*—are the thoughts of your subconscious mind and it's this part of your mind that houses every negative emotion you have ever experienced, and collectively these memories make up your emotional vibration. Because the subconscious memories play on a lower level to your immediate thoughts, you only catch them every now and then.

Tomorrow morning, see if this is true for you: the very second you wake up, you feel good—your body feels at peace. Then your conscious mind starts its scan of your body and surroundings. As you take note of your health, the room temperature, your level of fatigue at waking too early or at the right time... all of a sudden your subconscious mind starts playing the loop of emotional memories. You catch a few flashes of conversations here and there: a row with a co-worker, a relationship break-up, the time someone yelled at you, when you went into a rage... you're fully awake now and that first peacefulness is replaced with a heaviness that you can't quite shake. Most of us get up out of bed and go about our day and the subconscious shuffle of memories gets a little dulled when we focus on our conscious thoughts of getting to work on time, meeting our work deadlines, thinking of what to make for dinner that night. But the feeling is still there...

When my client, Rob, came into my room for his first appointment and I stepped into his body and became him, I picked up a darkness in his thoughts as if he didn't deserve to exist. The thoughts were low, on a suicidal level. Not only were they telling him he had nothing to offer the world, but they also affected his conscious thoughts by twisting any positive in his life into a negative.

Rob is not the first client to walk through my door with this problem. The negativity in the subconscious has a source, but years of its darkness can affect the conscious thoughts. The emotional vibration is belittling, creating a hopelessness for the person. Sometimes it can help to navigate the client to an overview of their life so they have the full picture of their life in a detached way, rather than through the negative lens. With Rob's base being overseas, and his sub-conscious creating suicidal thoughts, I needed to get to the crux of his issue quickly.

Emotional vibration: cause and effect

"Can you take me through your life; work, relationship, family life as it is it is for you now," I asked. As Rob answered this question, I became puzzled by the difference between the details he was telling and the feeling in his body—they just didn't add up. Rob's life sounded like one of the good ones. As we discussed the details of his life and business in Dubai, he highlighted the stress and hardships as failures, while I deemed his life as successful.

He owned property back at home in England, and had a close relationship with his family there. Again, he measured this as a negative; he didn't *own* the property as it had a mortgage and it was only *one* property while other businessmen had multiple investment properties. Even his close family relationships were negative because they lived on the other side of the world and they couldn't get to visit him enough. "I work so hard but I don't have enough to fly them out to see me more often." He flew them at least once, if not twice a year. He made out as if he should be flying them out every weekend! Even his personal life was successful; he was engaged to a beautiful woman and they were planning to get married shortly. His thoughts twisted this to a negative; he didn't understand why his fiancé Becky wanted to tie herself to him with his life in such a bad way.

Rob continued describing his lifestyle; his weekday routine often involved working late and then hitting the gym before going home, catching up with his fiancé over dinner. "I can easily ignore my downers on weekdays because my work keeps my mind occupied on problem-solving," he explained his business was in engineering. "It's the weekends and all that downtime that my bad thoughts start to creep back in."

Emotions can have a powerful effect on the direction you take in your life—Rob's subconscious mind was bringing him to the point of considering suicide. "Nothing unusual ever happened in my childhood, other than the usual teenage angst. I don't know where my dark thoughts are coming from. It's got so bad I can't look at myself in the mirror, I feel an overwhelming shame that I've wasted my life and my opportunities," Rob explained. "It's as if I'm running out of time to make it right. I'm so ashamed of myself, it makes me feel sick in my stomach all the time." The stress was affecting his health and he complained of psoriasis on his skin.

Understanding your emotions

Logically, Rob's problem doesn't make sense but then emotions never make sense and that's why they can overpower us. I always tell my clients to **look beyond the drama to the EMOTION the drama brings up in your body.** I've read the emotional vibration of thousands of different people over the past 20 years. Both positive and negative emotions work the same way, except negative emotions become dysfunctional or traumatic because they get trapped in your body. The reason being is that it simply isn't as easy to play out negative emotions as positive ones. Once it's trapped, a negative emotion will lay dormant until another incident activates it—this can happen over and over again. Each time it rises up to the surface it overpowers your whole body and your actions.

Think back to a happy time in your childhood. Do you recall a significant event, birthday or holiday that made you excited? Do you remember when your parents told you the event was happening? You may have counted down the days, your body was jumping with joy from all the excitement. The emotion taking over your body then was happiness. Happiness caused you to countdown the days, with anticipation and hope, until the event took place. Likely you also imagined or talked about all the fun things you were going to do at the upcoming event. When the day of the event finally came around, the event might have played out exactly, if not better, than your imagination had scripted it in your head. Fun and excitement adds to happiness which is fulfilled and performed, and so can easily pass through your body.

Traumatic emotions work in the same way, except they never completely play out so the emotion doesn't pass through and exit your body. Think back to a sad or traumatic event in your childhood. You might have witnessed your mother cut her finger in the kitchen. At the sight of the blood, you panicked. Your emotional reaction is fear. You projected this fear into a future scenario of death and loss of your mother, who you love most in the world. Adrenaline coursed through your body for the first time causing you distress. Your parents console you, saying, 'It's okay. Don't worry about it.' Their adult logic is trying to tell you it's okay without fully explaining it to you. It's not your parents' fault, that's what was said to them. At their insistence, you fight the emotion and push it down, locking it into your body where it will be activated in your adult life—again and again.

With no trauma evident in his childhood or life that would cause his suicidal thoughts, I went back into Rob's DNA to find the source of the emotion. I got a vision of a man, with Rob's characteristics, arguing with a woman—his wife it seemed—it became apparent that he was making a choice to stay and go to war in his country and she was choosing safety and leaving on a boat with the children. It's as if he was making the choice to stay with his brothers and fight for this country over leaving with his family. I asked Rob did he know his family history and if his grandfather had been involved in war. He spoke of a civil war in his grandfather's time in Ireland. I asked him to investigate—it's important to identify the origins of the emotional thread in order to heal it.

Emotional inheritance

The emotional dysfunction in your DNA isn't yours but it overwhelms you so that you will wake up and take notice of it—so you will finally do something about it. When you've had an emotional reaction that you don't know where it's come from, you put it down as a 'freak occurrence'.

If you're really honest, you are slightly worried that it isn't just a freak occurrence and it's actually part of your personality make-up that you need to be careful to control? You're not alone. **Every single person on earth has ancestry emotional dysfunction they have inherited along with their genetic body, and so do you**. When these dysfunctions are activated, they create an explosive reaction in your body that's so powerful it frightens you. After this 'big bang' of emotion calms down, you are left feeling like you're a bad person. This is because you don't understand where the emotions are coming from, so you take on the blame for the hurt you inflict on the people in your life with your behaviour. Without understanding how or why your body is having such powerful emotions, the guilt becomes a constant battle.

To cope with the yo-yo of explosive emotions, followed by unbearable guilt, your body uses a defence mechanism as a form of self-protection. It does this in one of two ways: pushing the blame outwards or pushing it downwards, so it doesn't have to face it. Basically, you either 'attack' the person that has activated the emotion, blaming them for it, so you don't have to take on the guilt; or you 'numb' the emotion, pushing it down before it explodes, so you don't have to feel it and take on the guilt.

When you attack, you point the finger and blame the person or circumstances as being the problem. Everyone is at fault, except you. Does this sound like you? Now is the time to be honest with yourself. When you numb, you recognise an emotion is about to rise up, so you quickly bottle and push it back down. You can be so good at this that it may now feel as if you don't have emotions. Does this sound familiar? Both of these reactions are natural in-built defence-mechanisms that keep your body safe from feeling the roller-coaster of emotional highs and lows.

Every human has emotional dysfunction and pain—if you're not feeling any emotions, it means you've successfully pushed them down into your body and they could be causing you a physical illness or symptom. If you're dwelling in your emotional pain and feeling miserable, you are just giving these emotions more power to control you—which all adds up to more problems and dramas in your life.

In Rob's case, his investigations into this trauma revealed that his grandfather had witnessed the argument between his great grandmother and great grandfather when he was an 11-year-old boy. His great grandfather had been in the Irish Republican Army at a crucial time in Ireland's history of freeing itself from British rule. Rob's great grandfather chose to let his wife and children go to another country while he stayed to fight. Doing so, he had justified his actions by declaring to his wife, in front of their children, that "I'm a man, I need to fight"; Rob's grandfather at 11 had wanted to stay with his father and was devastated by this turn of events in his family life. The trauma of losing his father and that he also couldn't stay because he wasn't a full man yet created a trauma in his body.

The emotion doesn't have logic, it can't reason that he is too young to stay with his father and still needs his mother's nurturing. Instead, the emotional trauma is locked into his DNA as *I'm not man enough*, which stayed and was passed through his bloodline to Rob's father and then into Rob's body, where it was activated and began looping in his subconscious, telling him *I'm hopeless at being a man* and *I'm not good enough*. Rob's father was a particularly stern man who wanted the best for his children and felt parenting them with discipline was better than love. In Rob, this activated the 'I'm not good enough' DNA emotion but it didn't in his brother. The emotional inheritance, of up to seven previous generations, is in you but it's not always activated—but knowing that this is possible will help you recognise the emotion as belonging to your DNA if it's activated in your children.

The purpose of your emotions

Right back at the beginning of human existence, we didn't start out living busy stressful lives. In fact, it was a simple life. We worked as a community, sharing tasks, to meet our basic needs of food, shelter, water and sleep. **Our emotions had been designed to make us responsive**, essentially to create a drama in the body so we would react to a danger and respond with an action: defending ourselves or fleeing for safety.

Think of fear and how it makes you react; your body is flooded with a massive injection of adrenalin to create a reaction of 'fight or flight'. This hormone helped your ancestors survive the wilderness of the caveman years, when danger was life-threatening. Fast-forward to today's world and the same adrenaline response is being activated in your body through stress on a regular basis. The dramatic reaction it requires in your body is taking its toll on your nervous system.

Life has sped up, and the busyness activates adrenalin more frequently than it was biologically designed for. You can look up the science of this online. When it is activated, you can't play it out as your ancestors did in the wild because it's not acceptable to 'fight' a boss, co-worker or anything that causes your adrenaline to go into overdrive. In the same sense, neither can you take 'flight' and run away. So you suppress it in your body, storing it until it is activated again by another stress-related scenario. Fear was not designed to be a response to your boss, nor was anxiety designed as a response to your bills. Instead of acting out your natural response to adrenalin, you numb it by going on autopilot or using a "reward" substance to cope with the stress of your busy life.

After I took Rob through the visualisation technique of giving the emotion back through the umbilical cord and then cutting the cord and sending the emotion and his family into space, we discussed his life. With the emotion no longer taking control of him, I highlighted the elements of his life as a success. I explained to him how the majority of people wanted his life; particularly the freedom and independence that came with owning their own business—I taught him how to measure the success of these elements in his life, rather than focus on the negatives. He acknowledged that all jobs came with stress but that being a master of his own work had the freedom and benefits most people only dreamed about. He started to agree with his successes—sure he didn't own 100 properties, but he wasn't a developer with high levels of risk and he was close to owning his own home— something that is becoming more and more unachievable to the average person. The fact his family wanted to spend time with him and he was about to embark on his own family life suddenly looked like a more colourful picture than its previous bleakness.

Since Rob had to return to Dubai and we couldn't continue our sessions, I knew he would have to work very hard to counteract his negative mindset. The original emotion was powerful but it had existed over a few generations and Rob had it running in his subconscious for years. While the emotion was unhooked, it would require him to constantly monitor it until a positive outlook became more dominant in his subconscious. It was now up to Rob to rewrite his subconscious from negative to positive. His healing had occurred while he was on holiday, the real test would be in his daily life when a stressful situation occurred and he reacted without being aware.

Since he couldn't return to me for a healing on those occasions, I gave Rob two important tools to help him improve his life: the first was to **check in with his body first thing every morning and bring his conscious attention to his emotional wellbeing**. The second tool was to focus on his response to stressful situations and how he dealt with them. The intention was to have these two checking points so that he could ground himself with the monitoring as his starting point to the day. I explained that the purpose of the second tool was to step away from the reaction and to realise the emotional response didn't belong to him, since it was part of his inheritance. The awareness of ancestral emotional inheritance means Rob doesn't have to feel the emotion and then add more damaging *I'm a bad person* thoughts to his already negative mindset.

How to make the correct decision

Today, you have the same two choices as Rob... you have these two choices in any given situation at any given time. You rarely take the correct option. Instead you tend to muddy the decision making with your adult logic that allows for morality, empathy for another's situation, difficulty in asserting yourself... whatever it is, you always find an excuse to justify a wrong decision.

If you take 5 minutes, right now, I will show you how to connect with your heart so you make the correct decision for yourself and humanity, at any given time.

1. Who do you love more than yourself? It's usually a child, it could be yours, a nephew, or

a niece. No child in your life? How about a sibling.... if you're not close to anyone, think of an animal. If there is no animal in your life, think of a favourite place that you love.
2. Now keep that person/animal/place in your mind. Let the love you have for them/it have full expression—imagine the huge cuddle you are going to give them when you see them or how full your heart feels when you're in your favourite place.
3. Hold that love there... if you lose it, go back to step 1 and bring the love back in.
4. With the love in your heart, ask yourself what is the correct decision to make to that difficult situation, from your heart.
5. That there is the correct decision for you and *your* experience. If your adult logic taints that decision, go back to step 1 and start the process over again.

Stop running: it's time to confront your emotions

Confronting emotions is not easy, particularly because your adult logic has an ego that doesn't want to admit it's wrong. Your body is confused by the negative emotions it inherited, so it uses a coping mechanism in the form of a character. You use this character to role-play in your life as if you were in a performance. If you didn't have this coping mechanism, you would have to face those negative emotions and that comes with too much uncertainty and pain. The benefit of the character is that you get to be the 'legend' of your life, where you can do no wrong. Your body reasons that it's safer to build a legend status, finding an excuse to put the blame elsewhere rather than face it.

Take a moment to think about which of these characters is you:

- *DRAMA QUEEN* Ugh, how hard is your life! The slightest thing makes you flip out and when it does, boy do you make sure everyone knows how upset you are. This character gives you legend status because no-one wants to upset you—you just make everything into too much of a drama, so people tiptoe around you or avoid you altogether.
- *WILD CHILD* You flip from one thing to another, you just can't stay still. The mundane life is not for you—no way that's for boring people. If you did stop for too long in any one place you would have to face up to your

dysfunctions, so better to keep moving! You become a legend because you're up for anything; the fun adventurous type with the interesting life. Oh but when issues arise, you quickly disappear.

- *VINDICTIVE* Everyone is against you... people are just horrible, corrupt and plain old nasty. They prove this time and time again. You just can't catch a break. This character makes you the legend because it helps hide the truth that you take comfort in your misery. It's easier to blame everyone else than face those difficult emotions in yourself.
- *MARTYR* Oh boy, do you love taking on other people's problems. Not everyone's, of course, you're careful to select those people who are worse off than yours so it makes you look better. You become the legend this way, because you get to look good. You get to be the caring, all-knowing one and nobody—including you—gets to see your emotional dysfunctions.
- *ATTENTION SEEKER* Look at me, look at me! Everything is about you, even when it isn't.

Making it all about you, means you get to be the legend. You get to control what people see, and you make sure it's the best version—no way will people see anything less than the best and brightest side of you.

- *WISE ONE* You know it all; you have the answer for everyone's problems. You like to dispense advice, even when it's not asked for. You have a reason for everything. Being the wise one gives you legend status because it means projecting outwards onto others so you don't have to look at your own dysfunctions.

Your character is stuck in its role-play

I warned Rob about his character and how it would challenge him with logic to thwart his efforts. It would become hard for him to recall the healing we had done in my clinic, to use the monitoring tools and recognise that his body was having the reaction—which is the sign that you know **an emotional problem is yours because you are the one reacting**. His vindictive character would play it out as the other person's fault and he would have to work very hard to keep his focus on why he was reacting, rather than getting caught up in the effects of the reaction. I knew he would return to Dubai and he would feel an initial uplift from unhooking the emotion but without using the daily monitoring tools, he would fall back into his negative mindset.

He had already told me his coping mechanisms were alcohol and drugs, so there was a real chance of him becoming dependent on them again to cancel out his thoughts, which would eventually lead to a deterioration in his business and relationships. The negativity might be kept at bay in his relationship because he lived a carefree life and he had the attention of his fiancé, but as soon as children are in the picture he won't have her focus and his 'not-good-enough' emotional negativity will cause him to react. He will row about this with his wife and it will create conflict in their relationship. With so much pressure on the relationship while they are rearing children, it could result in divorce. If he manages to get through divorce and a fledgling business life, he will come out of it in his 50s or so and the wisdom that comes with age may mean he will eventually settle his emotions, but he will have left a damaging effect on nearly everyone in his life.

Adapt to being uncomfortable

Emotions have a powerful effect on our bodies and that tends to cause us to run away from them, to ignore them in the hopes they will just go away. The initial gratification of escapism leads to its own kind of eventual difficulty. The human body does not like change. We like structure and for things to be a certain way, so much so that any change to our structure leaves us feeling off balance or uncomfortable. You know when children throw tantrums when there is a change to their routine? Well, adults are just the same—without throwing themselves on the floor, of course!

Here's how your internal tantrum can be triggered:

- How do you like your coffee? What happens when your barista changes your order or coffee blend?
- How do you like your bed? What happens when you sleep somewhere different? Not good, but you cope? You'll get back to your bed soon enough and all will be right.
- How do you like your car? It's great when it runs properly, but think of when there's a mechanical problem. How do you feel then?

- Your phone has got issues—how does it make you feel?

Now think about the things in your life that you don't like:

- Your job?
- Your living situation?
- Your social circle?

You could change them, there's plenty of opportunity to do that... but there's comfort in the familiarity, even though they annoy you. We just love structure, order and routine. When we go on holiday, we even set up routines for the duration that we are there. We say we love holidays but we also love coming home to our comforts.

We do not like change, it upsets the calm and orderliness of our routine. Yet, look how fast our world is changing—we now think nothing of connecting with a stranger on our mobile phones and then meeting them in person for a date, when we wouldn't have dreamed of it a few short years ago. We use our phones to transfer money instead of going into a bank. We wave a card at a gadget in a shop and it pays for our groceries, when not long ago it was only cash that was acceptable. We send messages to the other side of the world and get an instant response. This change is affecting our stress levels, making structure and order even more important to us.

I'm highlighting this fact because **if you're going to make transformations in your life, it will mean being uncomfortable some of the time**. It means stepping out of your routines and habits and looking at the character you've adopted to cope with life. This character is attached to these dysfunctions—it finds comfort in them. Confronting them means you will have to face up to your own deceit—yes, you've been tricking yourself.

How healing will affect your human character

The character you play in your life won't like it when it is forced to face the negativity it has helped create. It's possible you are not consciously aware of the character doing this, but if any of the above resonates with you or makes you cringe, then that is your character. When life brings you confronting situations it will rock this character and you will feel unsettled, uncomfortable and want to revert to blaming someone else—even me! Your character will try and battle with your new learnings and convince you to give up. Remember, our human bodies don't like changes to our structure. This is how the characters will react to change:

- DRAMA QUEEN The legend who turns everything into a drama, are you going to keep reacting to every little thing?
- WILD CHILD The legend who loves an adventure... and running away! How will you cope when drama arises through the healing? Your character will convince you to start running every time. Things get real = RUN!
- VINDICTIVE The legend that loves to point the finger at everyone else. This character loves the comfort of the misery, convincing you that it's safer, easier to shut out the world and stay at home away from it all.
- MARTYR The legend who helps others. What happens when you're exposed for having your own self-interests underneath that caring persona?
- ATTENTION SEEKER The oh-so-fun 'look-at-me' legend, what are you going to do when it's all about you for the wrong reasons?

- WISE ONE What happens when your emotional dysfunctions get exposed and you're no longer looking so wise?

Sadly, Rob didn't heed my warnings. The friend that put him in touch with me reported that his life is in a mess. His drinking got him into trouble with the Dubai police, which affected his business and may result in him losing his home and it will probably affect his relationship with his fiancé, if it hasn't already. You are given the same warning signs as Rob every day. **It's simple; if you are on the correct path, life will have a flow that's manageable.** If you are not following the correct path, your life will become very difficult.

Chapter 3
It's time to wake up!

When you've mastered the skills to get to the highest level in any game, your time and effort is rewarded with an advantage of space. This advantage lets you see the play coming in advance, giving you time to consider and respond accordingly. You can master your life in much the same way. With time and effort, you will move through levels that will eventually give you the advantage of space to see how the elements of your life are played out, who the key players in your relationships are, and who are not. The result is a wisdom that means that in any given situation in your life you can see the game plan and know how to play it to your advantage.

The levels of your life

Your life has a series of 'problems'—from the everyday to the more serious—which keeps you from mastering the game of your life. The reactions you have are what cause you the most problems—the stress, frustration, fear, anxiety, or whatever emotion it is that makes you react without wisdom, such as meekly agreeing to all of your boss's outrageous demands; or maybe you're the type that blows up into a rage at the slightest thing. These reactions take time—the boss who you fear creates a stress in your body and you spend more time at work, less time with your family. You end up annoying your family or partner and the consequence is the deterioration of your relationship and family life. You don't know what to do about it, so you work harder to appease your boss but the demands are always there and inevitably they lead to late nights that affect your home life. You have to do the work because you've got a family to feed and a mortgage to pay. This double whammy is how you get stuck in a rut, or feel helpless in your own life.

What if you could break the pattern of reacting to all your problems and clear the fog to gain a clear perspective of your life? It is possible to deactivate your emotions, and the more you do it on a regular basis the more you will alter your perspective. I call these different levels of healing 'dimensions'; which does not involve an actual physical destination, instead it's a change in your perspective that will help you to view the world and your life without reacting to it emotionally.

The everyday level: AKA 'the Third Dimension'

The daily grind with its groundhog day-to-day, week-to-week, month-to-month and year-to-year habits is called the 'third dimension'. Your life and thoughts in this dimension are aimed at meeting your basic human needs (food, shelter, water and sleep) and desires (big house, fancy car, etc.). In this day-to-day existence, we are often labelled according to our wealth: from poor to average or middle class to rich. Other labels include the level of education we have, our physical appearance, the suburbs we live in, the countries we come from, and the languages we speak. The majority of people are just surviving the day-to-day life, trying to get by.

Your human life has a rhythm that moves through stages: education (school and/or university), then career, marriage, family, holidays, retirement and, eventually, death. In between these milestones, you strive to fit in and gain ownership over something you think will satisfy your need for security and stability, but this sets you up for a merry-go-round of turmoil. Think about it:

- How do you live your life?
- How do the people around you live their lives?
- How many times have you 'wished' for a better life or wanted to fit in with someone else's way of life?
- Whose life did you want?
- Have you 'wished' you could afford all the luxuries that seem to come easily to others? What luxuries did you wish for?

Seeking 'happiness' causes sorrow

Wishing your life were better doesn't actually give you the solution to how you can make it better. You might focus on something you can do or afford right now that will make you happy. This might be small, like; *if I get the latest smartphone, then I'll be happy.* So you get the phone... And it probably does make you happy for a little while... Then life goes back to normal. Then, you think, *what else can I do to improve my life and make myself happy?* You might think; *a new TV will make me happy.* So you buy it with your credit card, adding more debt to your life.

The TV makes you happy for a while, but then your life goes back to normal again. Soon enough, you obsess over another material possession giving you the answer to your 'happiness' problem. Before long, your life is one big cycle of craving something to make you happy, creating more debt, then more stress to pay the debt, creating more desire to reward yourself in the hopes you can be happy again. This causes the relationships in your life to suffer because you need to work longer hours to earn money to pay for your 'happiness debts'. The consequence to you is your freedom, and it's why you are stuck in a rut.

Everyone has a colleague, friend or contemporary that boasts of their so-called successes when you bump into them, 'I've got equity', 'I've just bought my fifth property', 'check out my gold watch, I bought it to celebrate my promotion' ... they're excited because they're 'winning'... or are they? The gold watch is a status that their ego needs to represent 'success'. It's functional, sure, but so are less expensive ones. Equity is a positive spin that a bank uses to suck you into more debt... it doesn't translate to instant wealth. If you stopped and questioned your colleague or even yourself, as to why you need these things, you or they would realise that it's a bandage to patch up emotions, to make life a little glossier. Consider yourself lucky if you're one of the few who can really afford material luxuries—it probably won't cause you conflict—but the majority of us simply can't afford them. So many of us are living beyond our means, accumulating debt, and we are teaching our children to do the same. This desire for a 'better life' that we can't afford is causing damage through an emotional rollercoaster of envy and greed.

Living on autopilot

You didn't suddenly wake up one day desiring possessions to numb your pain; it's a gradual change that happens to you over the course of your third-dimensional life.

When you're a child, you don't understand the way the world works, so your thoughts exist in a fantasy world of make-believe. During your teenage years these thoughts become wishful—as you wish for the kind of life you'd like to live. Then in adulthood they become hopeful—as you hoped your life would get better. But during the day-to-day routine life of adulthood you get caught up in the 'rat race' and it becomes all too hard to break out of your Groundhog thought pattern. So you put your thoughts and emotions into a coma, where they exist on autopilot, getting from one day to the next. Every now and then your thoughts might come out of the coma and you will question your life, asking; *is this really it?* Or; *is there more to life than getting from day-to-day?* But it's often too hard to find the answer, so you push your thoughts and emotions back into the coma, living again on autopilot—getting from day-to-day; just surviving, hoping someone or something will come and rescue you from your everyday existence and give it more meaning.

From time to time, the question resurfaces into your awareness, but you know you don't have the answer so you learn to keep pushing it down because it becomes too painful to consider anymore. Before long, life passes you by and you end up on your deathbed, riddled with the emotions you've spent your life blocking. There, you think:

- What did I do with my life?
- Where did the years go?
- Why didn't I do that?
- Why didn't I say sorry?

- Why didn't I speak up when I had the chance?
- Why didn't I say I loved more?

Then, sadly, you will die without ever having achieved what your soul set out to achieve in this lifetime. I've seen it happen, over and over again.

Next level: Fourth-Dimension Minus"

The fact you are reading this book means you are a bit removed from the third dimension. The questioning of your third-dimension monotony might have come out of curiosity or a feeling of emptiness. I've had many a client who sought me out because they had heard of me through a friend and had been curious. For many it occurs after a shock to the system. Breaking my neck was my awakening and led me to Eileen, who thankfully set me on my path. You might have had your 'shock' through a similar accident, a relationship break-up, the loss of a loved one, experiencing profound grief, or a job loss. Whatever it is, it changes your perspective so drastically that it forces you to look at your life in a whole new way. This dimension is called the fourth-dimension minus and you know you are in it by questioning the elements in your life. It works like this:

- Do you feel like your life has fallen in a pit and you can't find your way out?
- Does it feel like you've hit rock bottom and you don't know what to do next?
- Did life make perfect sense to you before, but now these new thoughts are shaking your sense of who you are?

The first question you ask yourself is; *why is this happening to me?* The wake-up call that shocked you out of your everyday third-dimensional monotony caused this shift in your thinking, so now you are evaluating the meaninglessness of your day-to-day existence and you are looking for something to give your life purpose. It's as if the question, 'What am I doing with my life?' has become a big neon sign flashing in your face, forcing you to address it.

This sense of uneasiness or emptiness has come about because your circumstances, old habits, or things you thought were making you happy no longer do. When you move into the fourth-dimension minus way of thinking, you will seek out answers. Even if you didn't come to this level from a shock to the system, your curiosity is enough for you to start questioning. Doing this will put you in touch with healers, who I call 'soul-diers' because their soul is fighting the human dysfunction and winning. A soul-dier will throw you a lifeline so that you can find the answer to your questions for your life. My clients are soul-diers, as are healers on this earth whose purpose it is to help others—and they can come in all shapes, forms and occupations. One of them may have even handed you this book!

Next level: finding purpose
AKA 'Fourth-Dimension Plus'

You will naturally move from questioning your life to looking for answers to the meaning and purpose of it. When you come into this perspective, you realise that there is actually more to life than the everyday routine habits and activities that made up your existence in the third dimension. You will notice an increased awareness of your surroundings and the people in it. It's as if the fog lifts and you can see the relationships in your life for what they truly are. You find yourself in awe at this wisdom of knowing how the players in the life game are motivated and how you are now a spectator—mastering the game plan is just around the corner. Somehow you intrinsically know this, without being able to pinpoint how you know it. As you are gifted with this life wisdom, you will feel energised with new-found curiosity and purpose in your thoughts and decisions. This builds excitement and a natural desire to learn more, which will focus your beliefs and strengthen your intuition—like a mental telepathy—and attract new people and situations into your life. You need to use these people and situations to accelerate your healing—everyone has a purpose for being in your life, so tapping into the why and how will help you heal your dysfunctions and gain more perspective over your life.

Next level: The 'Fifth Dimension'

As you strip away your dysfunctional emotions with the healing tools, your thought patterns will change again. You will gain the ability to see your life with a bird's-eye view, which brings wisdom, knowledge and understanding about human life. You will have compassion for where other people are at in their life because their struggle is exactly like yours was before you began the process of healing.

This will make you humble. When you view the everyday world with the fifth-dimension way of thinking you can see that at our essence, we are really all equal on a level playing field. There is no hierarchy or superiority with this perspective. So the labels 'mother' or 'father', 'boss' or 'superior' that distinguish or frustrate us in our everyday life no longer carry such importance. You will realise we are all human beings, existing on earth together to learn our lessons. Even celebrities, politicians or people with the 'rich and famous' label have no greater value than people who collect our rubbish. Yes, really.

Your intuition and natural wisdom become stronger and you trust, more and more, that it will take you in the right direction. This new enlightenment means you step off the merry-go-round of the third-dimensional life and see the world and your life in it for what it is. Basically, you stop stressing about the small stuff—the everyday nonsense that seemed to clutter your life in the third dimension.

Now, **if you fall back into your old pattern of thinking, you can easily catch it and know there's something in it for you to learn and understand.** As your intuition becomes stronger, so does your urge to speak and seek out the truth with compassion for humanity. This empathy towards humanity comes naturally with an understanding that not everyone has access to his or her truth. When you learn to step into somebody else's shoes, you experience life from their point of view, rather than from just your own perspective—this removes all judgement, criticism and opinion that used to be a part of your thinking. In the fifth dimension, you have wisdom and you will find meaning and purpose for your life.

How to master your life

Your two choices haven't changed since I introduced them at the beginning of this book and they will never change at each level. Your two choices: take the easy option of running away from your emotions and end up in more difficulty in other areas of your life or take the harder option of confronting your emotions now and you will get out of your rut and master the life game.

Your biggest battle is within yourself

The biggest challenge you will have to face is your own truth. You have developed a character that is helping you survive the onslaught of emotion that makes you feel so bad everyday—I guarantee it will convince you that someone else, something else, anything else is at fault but you. It will do this in clever ways, it will make you so angry that you will blame the person who provoked you—even this book. It will reason with you that it's all too much, it's not possible to exist with turmoil and you need to go back to basics, where you were before. Your character is clever in its trickery but essentially it is lazy, it doesn't want to have to face the upheaval of emotion—the only option is to fight the feelings that tell you to give up. **Fight the fatigue, just keep confronting the emotions when they come up and find their source in your life**. Don't let yourself be convinced that you're not making progress.

Stay focused on the purpose

It's also possible you will get side-tracked, life can get pretty good in the fifth—so good in fact that you might be tempted to stay at that level not bothering to interact with the game players in the third because they are so tiring and caught up with all their many, many problems. But that's not how you master the game!

The game has to be lived in the third dimension with a fifth-dimension perspective. You will get exhausted explaining how to win the game to those around you that it will be tempting to give up on socialising with your third-dimension relationships. You are not a guru, you still have work to do so don't give up on your life. Those third-dimensional people are in your life to help you find your lessons and to heal.

Make healing a lifelong habit, and you will truly master the game of life. Getting to Fourth-Dimension Plus will give you a positive surge and healing will have a noticeable effect on your life; but like Rob in Chapter 2, without really working at it you will fall down harder than before. The fifth dimension is only part of the game—**to truly master your life, you have to check in on emotions every single day and heal them**. No running or hiding from your life. Put in the work every single day as a part of your daily routine and you will master the levels and, ultimately, your life.

Core battles: relationships, money and self-worth

Everyone's struggles will be different, so it's difficult to give you a story that will cover them all. After clearing a client's path, I put them into a maintenance phase where they can come and see me if there is anything major affecting them but they don't need to see me as often as they do when they first start out. In maintenance, my clients have learnt the tools so they only need to come back if a situation is too difficult for them to understand. Clients tend to have a range of dysfunctions they need to heal, but underlying that is a core issue. If I could narrow core issues down to a few, I would say the major three are money, relationships and self-worth—here's an example for each:

Katherine, relationships

When I did Katherine's reading, I could see her children really clearly but I couldn't see a husband. She explained that she was 33 and would like to find a relationship. After her reading, I sent her home to throw out her 'tokens'—you know the tokens you keep of the good times but lead you to remembering the pain? We all carry tokens because we like the good memory, but this good memory inevitably moves our thoughts from good to bad at what became a loss—so I call them memorials of your emotional pain! Getting rid of tokens clears the clutter in your life and **the act of throwing out the token allows your subconscious to throw out the memory.** It's cathartic and I recommend it to all of my clients to initiate their healing. A few sessions later, Katherine was excited to report that she had met someone—as the romance progressed it brought up issues which were beneficial and we deactivated the emotions. The romance ran its course and came to an end six weeks later. Over the course of five years, this continued to happen—Katherine would meet a man and never progress the courtship past the dating stage into a relationship. She would go through highs and lows when this happened. I knew it was her lesson, but she fought it hard. Her character played out the misery and told her that it came easy for others, why not her, and she was being punished. It would convince her to take the easy out, give up and blame anyone, everything else. Through the ups and downs, and as hard as it got—she persevered. Every end to a romance came with severe depression, but she carried on renewing her energies to continue dating. There was plenty of times she felt defeated but like a true *Soul-dier*, she carried on. She eventually got so far as moving out of the romance phase into a relationship with a long-distance partner. When it began to waver, she fought to keep the relationship intact. She learned to stand up for her own voice, by not excusing the behaviour of her partner. Unfortunately, it still ended. Awhile later she rallied again and met a new man who acted differently to the rest and was quick to progress the relationship. Despite some niggling doubts, Katherine allowed herself to get swept up in it. It seemed as if she had finally met a man who actually wanted a relationship! Unfortunately, cracks started to appear and at one little bump in the road he did a complete switch and ended it. This time Katherine didn't dwell in her misery or get depressed, she confronted him and explained his behaviour was not acceptable and he had conned her into thinking it was a committed relationship. Then Katherine had the strength to confront her own emotions and question her drive for a relationship. She realised her efforts had seemed difficult because they were out of her comfort zone but had really been half-hearted in finding a suitable partner. It was easier, she realised, to date the guy who 'wasn't that into you' because he wouldn't progress the relationship. Underneath her ego, the part of her character that wanted a relationship because that was what was expected of her, was the truth: she didn't really want to put the effort into a relationship. She realised then that she needed to make the choice to have one or not and then to live that life that was true to herself. This allowed Katherine to master her life instead of being at the mercy of her emotions.

Lucy, money

Money carries an energy with it, which isn't surprising given our lives are focused on it. If we have enough, we want more. If we don't have enough, we want more. Money comes easily to some and not so easily to others. When Lucy came into my clinic, she had a lot of problems all of which could be quite easily solved if she had more money. We explored her pattern with money and she had come from a large family, where money had always been tight. At first, the money pattern in her life seemed to be inherited from her parents but Lucy herself ran a successful business, in which she earned a decent amount of money. It became apparent that the core lesson in her life was money and it came through her husband. At the beginning of her marriage, Lucy's husband had run a successful business and there was plenty of money. Having missed out on money in her childhood, Lucy treated the money as never-ending and spent it as quickly as it came. She used her child-rearing years and husbands money to invest in courses to develop her skills. She also put more demands on her husband to earn more money to put into her business ideas. To try and attract the right clientele, she insisted her husband set up a home with a shop front in an affluent area. This added a lot of pressure to her family's finances. If Lucy had drilled down to her reasoning, her motives were not to attract clientele—she could do that anywhere—it was to live the high life. This lesson cost her and her family a lot. Her husband's business was undercut by bigger businesses and he couldn't meet the obligations of the new rental. They were forced to move, but they couldn't move back into their family home because the tenants were resisting eviction and fighting it through the courts. None of their families had the room to take them in, so for six months Lucy and her husband and kids were forced to live out of one room at her friend's home. On top of that, the tax department investigated their business accounts and found fault and fined her $80,000. Eventually Lucy and her family could move back into their home, but the tenants had done a lot of damage. Her husband was forced to take a job, and Lucy had to build her business up from home. By the time she came to see me her marriage was suffering; she was earning the majority of the household income and paying the bills. She was getting frustrated with her husband's inability to earn money. He was blaming her for putting them in financial ruin with her selfish desires and the relationship had stalemated. We worked on healing the dysfunctions she had inherited around money and it had a positive effect on her ability to bring in money. While money came easily enough through her business pursuits, it didn't alter her husband's ability to earn money. Where he had been affluent at the beginning of the marriage, he could only earn so much now. At first Lucy accepted the burden of being the majority earner as a lesson for her complacency but she expected her husband to do the majority of the household chores. When he didn't perform these well, they would row and her resentment would build. She learnt that being the breadwinner was unusual to her and that this led to her resentment. As a woman, who came from a long line of women who had men support them, it felt unnatural to be the breadwinner. Lucy persevered through the highs and lows. Rather than work for an employer, her husband attempted to re-establish his business again, but now, instead of a steady stream of income he had little-to-no income at all. This sent Lucy off on a course of resentment all over again, adding more pressure to her own business to try and earn even more money. His inability to earn money and her stress at paying every bill put a huge strain on the marriage. Through it all, Lucy persevered. She would go through bouts of working extra hard to earn the money to avoid feeling stressed about bills—this would cause her to get sick and be forced to take time off, which ultimately added more stress. This would then add to the resentment she felt towards her husband and they would row and it would add more stress to her life. Eventually she realised that she needed to change her habits around money; despite being the majority earner she would still 'reward' herself and buy things without thinking. She would go through exercise habits and diet fads buying all the new equipment, reasoning that she had all the stress of earning the money so she should have the rewards of it too. She changed this habit and stopped spending so much on 'rewards' which helped her neutralise some of the stress. She learnt to accept her breadwinner status for what it was and that in some ways it benefited other areas of her relationship. She found when she changed her habits and respected her money more, she saved—it sounds simple but it's not something she was used to doing—which lessened the stress on her so she could take a day off and her health improved naturally. Instead of reacting, Lucy mastered the game of her life.

Zac, self-worth

When Zac came to see me, it was out of curiosity. He'd had a major overhaul in his life around relationships but he'd found out about my work via a business colleague long after the dust had settled on his divorce. He was onto his second marriage and now had four children, two from his first and two from his second. When I explained the inheritance of emotions in his DNA, his response was 'great, let's fix it' and he wanted to come every day to get 'rid of their crap'. I explained healing wasn't a quick fix and if he was up for it, I could get him to a place where he could heal himself. Zac's a proactive guy, so he dutifully learnt everything I could teach him and applied it to his life. He had been born to wealthy parents' and had every advantage they could afford to give him but his self-worth is tied to their approval. His divorce had been difficult and still left him bitter, particularly because his parents didn't approve of him giving up on his marriage. We discovered through the healings that the failings in his first marriage had happened in his parents' but they'd kept their marriage going. This rallied Zac's urge to 'get rid of their shit' but underlying his efforts was their approval, making his core issue about self-worth. Zac had a lot of ambition; his first career was as a practitioner but that didn't satisfy his ambitions so he focused on the business end of it. When that failed to satisfy his ambition, he switched into a completely different industry where he had more success. This led to a hunger to set up his own company again, so he formed relationships to create a business where he could grow it and create a franchise chain. At every level he encountered problems in his business venture that would stall his efforts and leave him frustrated at the lack of progress. At each problem, he would go through a series of getting angry, blaming everyone around him but he persevered and eventually he realised that his drive for success in business was really to have his parents' approval; once he gained this perspective it lessened his frustrations and eased his burden. His business frustrations no longer felt like failures and he didn't react to things with as much anger. Zac's new perspective let him master his game plan and his life and business began to flow without difficulty.

What is the purpose of your life?

Your soul has a purpose for the life you are currently living. Its purpose can be anything and is often very simple. It might be to experience what it's like to live a life as a woman in a small village in Russia; or to experience the adventurous life of a male firefighter in New York.

The soul wants peace, but the human body it inhabits carries emotional dysfunction, which can create emotional reactions. Meaning, you may abandon the intended path of a humble life in a small village for fame and fortune as a ballerina, or instead of being a grounded New York firefighter, you pursue a nomadic life. Steering your life away from its intended path may not necessarily seem like a bad choice, but it's not right for your soul's purpose and the result of this is derailing your life.

Essentially, your life becomes a struggle; instead of living an easy life in a Russian village, you might struggle to become a ballerina. This struggle adds more dysfunction to your human life, creating more complications. Have you ever moved your life to a different area, state or country and found it difficult to settle into a rhythm? Sometimes one or two of the big items—work, home, relationships—in your life might be good, but they don't always flow together. Sometimes the reverse is possible, you become unsettled and venture off for a different life and find that your new location helps your life to flow, which means if things are not flowing for you then you are not on the path you need to be on.

When your life has harmony, and is flowing easily, it's a good indication you're in the right situation for you. I've seen many of my clients trying desperately to stay in careers and relationships that are simply not right for them and as soon as they use the healing tools, the struggle disappears. You will know you are on the right path for your soul when your life flows without complication.

You and I, we're the same

Often, I'm given visions of humanity at different stages over the long history of our human evolution. When I see these visions of human life from the first of us on earth to the billions of us today, it's very apparent that we have lost a connection or understanding of our original purpose for living a human life. Your soul has a game plan that's larger than your current human life; it's on a mission to understand the full experience of life on earth in human form. That means it needs to experience what it's like to live as every single race—so you could be Caucasian reading this, but in another life, you might have been Asian, African, European or such. Your soul has also been a female and a male, many times over. It has experienced a life of riches, the misery of poverty and everything in between.

The recipe of 'YOU'

Your life as it currently stands today is made up

of your human body, which includes seven generations of your ancestor's emotional DNA—in order to cope with this emotional blueprint, your current body developed a character to make sure the recipe always comes out as 'legend'—both of these human body ingredients have defects that end up derailing your soul from its intended journey. The YOU recipe also includes your soul, which has had its own lengthy journey before mixing itself into the human body of 'YOU'…

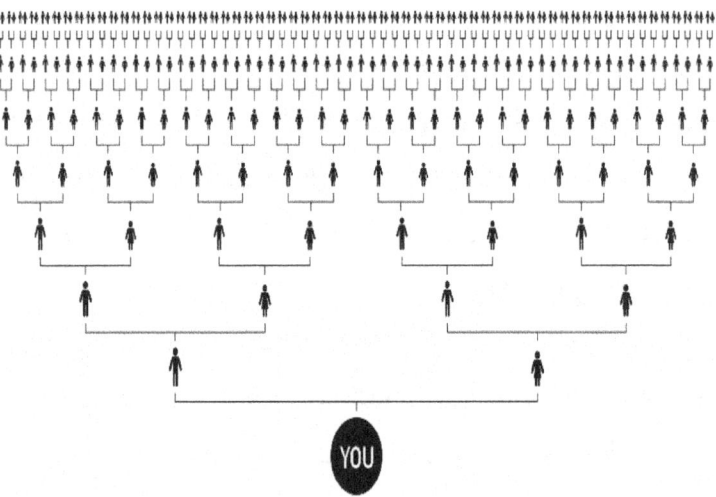

The soul journey

Your soul comes from a collection of billions of souls that are not individual but are all ONE and the same, called 'Source'. Imagine Source as a cloud in the sky and a soul as the raindrop that breaks away, dropping to earth and forming a part of the ocean, a puddle, a lake... Just like the raindrop, when a soul separates from Source to come into YOU, it still carries an element or essence of Source with it—which means this is also part of the recipe of YOU. At Source, all souls are <u>one</u>. Human words like 'completeness' and 'euphoria' are close to the idea of what it's like, but no words can really do justice to the complete wonder of this feeling. It is like that cosy contented belonging feeling you get when you return home—imagine that feeling magnified a gazillion times. Imagine coming home, taking off your human suit with all its fear, worry, anxieties and troubles and basking in the warmth of comforts that fill you with peace, love and contentment. Well, your soul knows this feeling well and it has a fierce longing to return 'home' to Source.

As ONE, Source holds the information from the experience of all human lives, right from the beginning of humankind to now. Your soul carries the wisdom of this collective human experience so that on its journey into human form, it can access it and stay on the right path to fulfil its mission quickly.

At the very beginning, this wasn't as complicated as it is for human lives today. Humanity came into earthly existence uncontaminated; we were raw, with no dysfunction. For those initial years, life was simple: we lived, we learned and we died. We followed our lessons easily because the connection to our spiritual body and the wisdom of Source was clear.

Over time, and many centuries of existence, with dysfunction added to dysfunction, our connection to Source became clouded and harder to tune into. Initially, we recognised the threat of this disconnection and the danger it presented to humanity's mission so we created 'religion' to remind us of our connection and keep our focus on our purpose. We made rules to remind us of what we needed to focus on. Some of us were deemed more enlightened and better at focusing on our purpose than others, so humanity agreed that the enlightened few should be appointed as our spiritual leaders to guide and keep us righteous. Sadly, those appointed leaders added more confusion with rules of their own. Soon enough our free will was affected by the fear that was created from the idea of a vengeful God—a name we had created for Source. The fear and guilt worked to contain some of us who kept following, but many more of us became doubtful of any religion that attached rules and regulations to God. This meant that humanity became divided in our beliefs, which has only added more layers of dysfunction to our earthly existence.

Fast-forward to today and God is no longer a word that makes us think of oneness or unity. Instead religions have divided us, created war, hatred and mass killings. The word God is tainted—it no longer reminds us of its true meaning of love, oneness and joy. Now 'God' means fear, hatred and control. For those of us living in countries without religious warfare, God brings up a negative image of religious enthusiasts trying to convert us to their beliefs. For those of us who do subscribe to a religion, we feel we can't speak of God, for fear of being judged.

We need each other now more than ever

But what is the real, uncontaminated meaning of God? 'God' is a name we use to symbolise or refer to our connection to our truth. God is our Source, where each soul comes together as one, and where each soul returns to at the end of a human life. God is oneness.

If humanity is like an orchestra, imagine us singing as one, as if we just fit in unity—our voices complementing and working as one to create a harmony. If even one performer or member is out of tune with the rest, it affects the harmony of the others and creates discord. This is what has happened to humanity. Through evolution and centuries of dysfunction, we are now disharmonious. We can't even agree to what sheet of music we should be singing from!

It is only in human form that we are divided, where the emotional DNA we inherit with our human body causes us to separate, so that we feel isolated.

Once your life is derailed from your soul's intended path, more problems arise at every wrong turn. Soon enough you're making choices that become a spider web of more bad choices. When your soul gets completely lost in human dysfunction, it can't tap into the wisdom of Source to find the right path. The mission of your soul is to have an experience of a life on earth, not to have a difficult life full of emotional trauma—yet that is what's happening to your life, to all lives.

I've seen souls leave human life and become spirit, who then carry these human dysfunctions back to Source. I was given a vision of this journey and it was as if they were quarantined at Source, very much like a customs checking area. The soul was surprised it carried baggage from the human life it had lived and was further dejected to realise it wasn't allowed back into Source until it could get rid of the emotional baggage it had acquired because the purity of Source can not be contaminated by emotional dysfunctions.

Take note; all those emotions you don't heal, inherited or acquired, that you carry through your lifetime don't die with your human body. Meaning, **your soul can't go 'home' so the only option is to return to another human life to heal the emotions**, so that your soul can finally complete the 'mission' and return to Source. This can happen over and over again, through hundreds of lifetimes.

We need every single member—no matter what race, nationality or sex—to help each other through the journey, so that we can come together as one again at Source. Every member of humanity contributes to the human experience—so accessing this pool of truth will bring you great wisdom, as if you had lived millions of human lives. This wisdom enriches your three-dimensional life because it allows you to step out of your life drama and look at it from a fifth-dimensional perspective with a bird's-eye view; where you just *know* the right thing to do in any situation, for the betterment of humankind. Healing your life will have a knock-on effect and will help each member in humanity's orchestra re-tune, so we can all come together and be ONE again.

Chapter 4
Confront your emotions and you will master life

Issues for me might seem insignificant to you, while something that makes you react with rage might seem trivial to me. And therein lies the clue to mastering the emotional game... if it's significant for you, as in you just found a parking fine on your windscreen and you don't think; *damn, should pay more attention. Ugh, what a waste of money could have spent the money on something nice...* as you get on with your day. If, instead your emotions blast into full rage as if your very existence was compromised by the parking fine; *O-M-G! WHAT-the-actual-f@#k. I can't DEAL with these inspectors .... Why doesn't the government focus on real criminals!* Followed by red-faced rage that doesn't dissipate after the initial shock, that's a sign of a dysfunctional emotional mindset that you need to work on healing.

Incidentally, this isn't the reaction of Lucy back in Chapter 3, who, if you recall, had the core issue of money. This is actually Zac's reaction—he parked illegally and then raged when he was issued with a fine. See, Zac would be the first one to get up in arms if someone else committed the same misdemeanour and it affected him—so his dysfunctions have him living with one set of rules for himself and another for everyone else. A reaction like this is the tip of the iceberg… you know, that tip of ice that sticks out of the water but attached to it underneath the ocean surface is a mountainous volume of ice. Your emotions are the same; what's on the tip is only a small indication of what lies beneath.

Map the emotion to find the cause

The dysfunctions you inherited through your DNA send out a frequency that brings people into your life to trigger these emotions; which is supposed to bring your focus to the reaction in your body. **It's the reaction that holds the clue to your core emotion**. In the case of the parking fine or another situation that triggers an explosive emotion like anger, the focus shouldn't be on the drama in a situation—how the world is against you—but on *why* that person or situation causes the response in *you*. The essence of your soul brings peace and love into your body; anything else is a dysfunctional emotion that doesn't belong to you so you need to heal it.

Mapping will help you retrace the pattern in your life until you find the original source of the emotion. Your subconscious memory has hoarded every detail of every emotional reaction you have ever experienced and will guide you when you give it the time and space to follow the path to its origin. It will take you back through the memories until you find the original trauma. Take it step by step, letting it unfold naturally, no matter how long it takes. I teach my clients the tools to do this for themselves because I firmly believe that you don't need me, or anyone else, to guide you—you know your own emotions because you've been living with them for your whole life. You're also the expert on your family's history and the emotions in your DNA—I guarantee your memory will guide you to the core emotion, if you give it time.

I asked my client, Natasha, to describe how she mapped an emotion to find its origin. Natasha has a partnership in a company, which is a relatively new experience for her, having previously spent her working life as an employee.

Natasha*:* 'My partner recently investigated a new business venture for the company and pitched it to the board. I had a terrible feeling about the idea, like it would get me into really big trouble. It felt really strong, as if this was make or break, so I couldn't agree to it. I rationalised my doubt to my partners and put it down to ethics. My colleagues thought I was crazy, they couldn't understand why I would veto it. I became really adamant that no-way could I possibly go down that road... I couldn't be budged on it. We stalemated at the meeting because no-one could make me consider it, I flat out would not do it. Logically, I knew this business venture made sense for the company and we were unlikely to get in trouble but I couldn't kick the very strong sense that I would get into trouble if we pursued it. I mulled it over for a while... or 'sat with it' as Leanne likes to say. My technique for this is to visualise the problem separately, as if I'm observing it in a bottle. Every time I thought about the reaction in the bottle, I knew it didn't make sense. From a business perspective, the idea was a great direction for the company and plenty of others were doing it. I went backwards through my life to see if the emotion had sprung up anywhere else. Nothing. Sure, I'd probably got into trouble when I was younger but nothing that left me with such a strong sense of doom like this would really get me into BIG trouble. So I knew then that this emotion didn't belong to me and it was inherited. When I had the time, I lay on my bed and connected to my heart, from there I brought up the emotion and visualised my parents standing in front of me. I didn't feel the pull to either of them so I knew it didn't belong to them. I visualised my mother's parents standing over her shoulder, side-by-side, and then I felt the strong pull towards my grandmother. Her life story is very vivid and had been told to me many times. Granny had been a very young girl in Lebanon, about 4-years-old, when her mother had died and she was placed into a boarding school because her father couldn't look after her. In those days, it had been a very cold, non-nurturing environment so I knew this feeling of getting into trouble had come from my grandmother and the experience of being sent away. I knew that the childish mind wouldn't have understood that it wasn't her fault and would have felt as if she was getting into trouble. To be sure I had hit the right emotion, I scanned my dad and his parents but I couldn't feel a reaction. My body responded strongly to my mum's side and my granny so I knew it had originated there and had been locked into the DNA and was now activated in me.

****

As Natasha did, locate the source of your emotional dysfunction then bring the emotion to the surface by baiting it. The dysfunctional emotions in your body were stored at a time when they were HUGE for you. To get them out, you need to make them HUGE again. The best way is to bait them or provoke them until they take over your body. This will allow your body to really feel them—instead of pushing them back down as it usually does—so you can get behind the emotion and finally *get it out* of your body.

See Appendix A for visualisation techniques and then follow these steps to bait your emotion:

- Start by visualising the emotion as if you were a child. With no rational thought, just *feel* the emotion.
- Catch the feeling and hold it
- Now bait it by exaggerating it: If it's jealousy, visualise your partner with another person. Exaggerate this scenario and make it really BIG. Think of the worst-case scenario; maybe your partner runs off with this other person and leaves you sad and lonely. Maybe you catch them together...

- Be really dramatic—this is the best time in your life to be as dramatic as you like
- If you were a child feeling this emotion, how would you give it expression? Allow the emotion to naturally build. Give it free reign to be as big as possible. You can help this by stomping your feet, or rolling around on the ground in a fit with flailing arms—if that's where the emotion wants to go, let it. (Remember, it's your mind's eye—not your real self. You can give the emotion full expression in your mind's eye without moving your physical body.)
- Feel the stress of the emotion taking over your whole body
- Stop
- Now locate *where* it is in your body; is it in your chest, stomach... *feel* it there.

Remember when an emotion rises from its hiding place in your subconscious to a conscious level, when it's in your everyday thoughts, your adult logic will try and talk you out of feeling the emotion. Don't listen to this logic—let your body feel the emotion by making it as large as possible. **These emotions are not logical—they were stored in your body when you were a child.** As a child they were BIG, so they need to be big again to heal them.

Even if an emotion has been inherited, it has the same childish effect in your body. Your adult logic will put reason to these emotions and push them back down again. This is what you've done for years, and your ancestry has done for hundreds of years. Don't allow your adult logic to talk you out of feeling the full strength of an emotion that needs to be healed. Your mind can be lazy and it likes structure and routine, so it's possible it will try and make you feel tired—or talk you out of it by telling you it's a stupid idea or it's already been healed. This is how your mind suppresses emotions to stop them from rising to the surface because feeling it is painful.

Remember, it hasn't been healed if a person or situation is triggering the feeling, even if you apply logic and convince yourself not to react. That's a short-term solution and Source will find another way to bring it to your attention. Be aware of this as you use the tools. Take it slow if you have to, but don't stop once you start. You need to keep going until all the original emotion, and any other emotion attached to it, is completely out of your body.

Sometimes an emotion can break and still live on—just like a worm's body will still live and grow when it's cut. If this happens, the emotion will still affect you. It's very important to be patient with your healing sessions and keep going until *all* of the emotion is out of your body.

Good riddance; time to push that emotion out

Tip: Speak this next passage aloud into a voice recorder, then play it back as you do the healing allowing your voice to guide you as you concentrate on the visualisations—just as my voice would guide you in my clinic.

[START]
- Come into your heart.
- Feel your heart.
- Stay in your heart as you do the healing.
- Now, recall the emotion overpowering your body. Bait it again if you have to.
- Feel the emotion, but don't take it on.
- Visualise your parent (either your mother or father whose DNA carried the inherited emotion) in front of you.
- Look over your parent's shoulders and see all of their ancestors, from their mother's side and all of their ancestors from their father's side—lining up,

one behind each other, as far as your eye can take you, right from the beginning of their existence. Even if you've never met these people before, feel them there. Pretend they exist. Come back to your parent. See an umbilical cord that is connected to you and your parent.

- Come into your heart. Using your heart's voice, with strength and force, tell your parent that you will neither accept, nor inherit or claim any dysfunction to do with [the emotion you are healing].
- Tell your parent that you will not take this dysfunction on, nor will you inherit it or claim it. You will not allow your future children, their children, or any future ancestors to inherit it.
- Visualise yourself using a tool as you tell your parent with your heart's voice, 'I will not accept any of this dysfunction. I will not have it in my system, or in my DNA.'
- Then let go of everything that you've ever experienced with the emotion, visualising it going through the umbilical cord that is attached to your parent and you. Letting it all go back to where it came from. Back through all your ancestors, back to the beginning.
- Take every memory, every thought, and feel them leaving your body. Feel the emotion going.

- Feel it all leaving your body.
- When it's gone and you can't feel the emotion, cut the umbilical cord between you and your parent, allowing them and all of their ancestors to float up in the air. Telling your parent, 'I love you, but I will not accept this.'
- Feel them floating up into the air, disappearing into the sky.
- Now visualise your other parent in front of you.
- Look over their shoulder and see all of their ancestors from their mother and father, lining up one behind each other as far as your eye can take you—right from the beginning of their existence. Even if you haven't see these people before, feel them there. Pretend they exist.
- Come back to your other parent, knowing that all of her ancestors are behind him/her.
- Feel an umbilical cord between you and this parent.
- Using your heart's voice with strength and conviction, tell them, 'I will not accept, nor will I inherit any dysfunction to do with [the emotion you are healing]'.
- Tell them, 'I will not accept [this emotion], nor will I inherit [this emotion], nor will I claim it. I will not allow my future children, my grandchildren or future ancestors to inherit [this emotion].'

- Take every memory, every thought to do with this experience and feel it leaving your body. Feel it all leaving your body.
- When it's gone and you can't feel any emotion but your heart's happiness, cut the umbilical cord between you and your parent, allowing them to float up in the air. Feel your parent and their ancestors floating up into the air. Tell your parent, 'I love you, but I won't accept any of this.'
- Feel them floating into the sky, and let it all go.
- Now come back into your body, into your heart and allow your soul to break out of this broken body.
- Let your soul come above your body and rise up into the heavens and allow Source/God to nourish your soul and give you strength, compassion, wisdom, patience, abundance and joy.
- Take these tools and allow these tools to nourish your soul.
- Thanking Source/God, come back down to earth, walk through a tunnel, walk to the end of this tunnel.
- Let go.
- Visualise a white door at the end of the tunnel.
- Open it and step into your new body—letting go of the past.
- See yourself in 5, 10, 20 years' time and so on… just enjoy letting go.

[END]

Note: You're not harming your parents in this healing; it is just a way of tricking your subconscious mind into letting go of its attachment to the inherited emotion.

Not sure which parent-ancestor line? Use this healing

Tip: Speak this next passage aloud into a voice recorder, then play it back as you do the healing allowing your voice to guide you as you concentrate on the visualisations—just as my voice would guide you in my clinic.

[START]
- Come into your heart.
- Feel your heart.
- Stay in your heart as you do the healing.
- Now, recall the emotion overpowering your body. Bait it again if you have to.
- Feel the emotion in your body, where is it sitting in your body? Go to the emotion, as if you can see it from behind.
- Now from that feeling, visualise your mother and father in front of you. Which parent stands out more? It might be both, but one will be stronger

than the other. This is the parent you have inherited the emotion from.
- Visualise the parent the emotion belongs to. Push this parent aside. From the feeling of being behind the emotion, you will see a number with your mind's eye. Recognise this number as how many generations of your ancestry have this emotion.
- Your body will identify a number. Trust it.
- Your body will feel a surge of emotion—a cluster of them. Don't allow your body to take these emotions on—they are part of the ancestors' dysfunction.
- Find a healing instrument (a super-powered hose, an axe—whatever you like) from your toolbox that your body feels comfortable using, and apply it to the emotion to get it out of your body.
- Put the emotions you just got out of your body into a box and hand it over to them. You will feel a release and love coming into your body.
- Now come back into your body, into your heart and allow your soul to break out of this broken body.
- Let your soul come above your body and rise up into the heavens and allow Source/God to nourish your soul and give you strength, compassion, wisdom, patience, abundance and joy. Take these tools and allow these tools to nourish your soul.
- Thanking Source/God, come back down to earth,

- walk through a tunnel, walk to the end of this tunnel.
- Let go.
- Visualise a white door at the end of the tunnel.
- Open it and step into your new body—letting go of the past.
- See yourself in 5, 10, 20 years' time and so on... just enjoy letting go.

[END]

Your go-to defence: are you attacking or numbing?

Zac and Lucy's self-protecting defence mechanism is to go on the attack and focus the blame outwards on a person who triggered the emotion. Attacking the person who activated the emotion in you means you blame that person for it, so you don't have to take on the guilt.

Natasha and Katherine numb as their defence mechanism. They recognise an emotion is about to rise up, so they quickly bottle it and push it back down so it doesn't explode with a burst of emotion because they feel an incredible sense of guilt afterwards. This numbing may feel as if you are not in touch with your emotions. **To heal, you need to feel the emotions** rise up and there is a way to get this process started.

One of the most effective tools is to de-clutter your home of the tokens and rubbish that are part of your old way of life. This will help you make the fresh start you need for your new life of healing. Tokens are the items you keep that represent your emotional baggage.

Are you hoarding your painful emotions?

Do you keep a memorabilia box full of love letters or special gifts given to you by people who you no longer have a relationship or friendship with? I think of this as a 'memorial' box since these tokens represent people who are no longer a part of your life—so why keep the reminder? These tokens represent your emotional baggage, which remind you of a painful time in your life. Even if they were given to you at a good time in the relationship, they will just remind you of the hurt that ended it. The bad memories in your subconscious play on a loop, adding to your emotional vibration that weighs you down so that you feel depressed, anxious, and unhappy. Painful emotional memories weigh you down, and prevent new people and situations from coming into your life. It's time to let go of all your tokens and emotional baggage.

Remove memorabilia

Ransack your home and get rid of any reminder of your past emotional pain to do with relationships, friendships, finance or anything that causes stress in your body. Tokens can be letters, gifts, photographs, concert tickets, gadgets, clothes, etc. Even throw out those broken items you've been meaning to repair that are only cluttering your home. Shred old documents and recycle the paper. Throw every token out, donate them to charity, or just give them away.

Follow the emotion

As you're de-cluttering, pay attention to any emotions that rise to the surface as you look at each item. Tune into your body and take note of any emotions so that you can come back to them later when you're ready to heal them. It's possible that you will become more emotional as you throw out your tokens—this is a natural effect of de-cluttering emotional baggage. Make notes and keep them for when you need to map an emotion. If you don't feel any emotion as you de-clutter, don't worry, they will come up for you later on when the time is right. Your conscious mind knows that these things are in the past, but your subconscious mind doesn't. De-cluttering will trick your subconscious mind into believing the emotion has gone into the bin, or simply been given away. Remember, regularly de-cluttering your living spaces is good for your soul.

Universal communication

De-cluttering will bring people and situations into your life to activate your emotions. This will seem like events in your life are conspiring against you at first, but really it's the exact opposite. Pay attention to the people, situations and other messages Source/God brings into your life. Analyse everything that happens to you—this will help strengthen your intuition and your ability to communicate with Source, which is important for your healing. Only you can really know how Source communicates with you—it depends on you and the senses you use to pick up these messages. These can be subtle, but if you haven't been paying attention they will become loud and re-occurring. My clients Emma and Heath volunteered to describe signs they received.

Emma: Just before I started doing the healing work, I had an argument with a friend. Let's call her Liz. I'd been feeling for a while that I didn't get a lot out of the friendship. If I was going to be brutally honest, I recognised that I kept Liz around because she filled a void. If I had no-one else to talk to, she could be guaranteed to answer the phone. In return, I put up with her negativity about nearly everything. Things came to a head when I met another group of friends I had a strong connection with. At the same time, Liz was planning her wedding and her negativity levels about this went to an all-time high. I could go into the details of this negativity, but she had always been like that from the get-go and I admit I'm at fault for continuing a friendship I didn't enjoy because it suited me as a 'just in case'. If I was to balance this story and ask for her input, she would agree. I was the friend who would say I'd come around and then either not bother or arrive super late. I'd borrow the extra car, which she most likely offered to be nice, and then have difficulty making the time to return it. I knew it was adding to her negativity but she never called me out on it, so I didn't fix my behaviour. Liz did once grumble about the lateness, which made me realise I was being too relaxed so I did fix that. The wedding plans were in full swing but the writing was on the wall when the interstate engagement party and international wedding location meant more investment emotionally and financially than my current shitty 'sometime' friendship stance—so I opted out. I didn't completely disappear, but I pulled back. I get now that this idea was more for my benefit than Liz's. I flagged my busy schedule to her in advance, hoping that it would be enough for her to get the hint. But it didn't work. The ignored calls and late-reply messages only exacerbated Liz's bitterness. It all came to a head when someone tagged me in a Facebook post and she could see I wasn't as 'busy' hiding away working as I'd made out. She added a bitter comment to the thread and the guilt made my anger flare. I called her in a rage and we had it out. I screamed all my anger and frustration at her about her negativity, she just couldn't understand how I'd gone from calling her regularly to nothing at all… my anger couldn't be contained and I yelled, 'I never want to see you again' and she hung up. Her fiancé tried to reason with me via text that 'admittedly she has a bad delivery but she meant well' but I'd had enough and told him I was done. Afterwards, and before I'd begun the healing work, I only felt bad that I had maintained a friendship that I didn't feel that strongly about. I reasoned that the showdown had only been necessary because she had gotten so clingy—as if caring was a fault. As I began the healing work, when an emotion was coming up I would cross paths with Liz. I can't be sure if she ever saw me on those occasions but she would be out running and literally cross my path. Sometimes it seemed as if she was in the strangest of places at the oddest times. I began to realise that she served a purpose in my life; as a reminder of my old broken path and that I needed to continue with my healing. The last time Liz crossed my path in what seemed the most unlikely place for her to be in, was just after I'd had another potential friendship break-up situation with a friend who had become very negative. Except this time, I worked at it with the healing tools and turned it around. I was with that friend, and a few others, when Liz ran past me. I took it as a sign of how far I'd come with my healing. While there isn't anything I can do to rectify my bad behaviour with Liz, I genuinely felt as if I'd achieved a milestone by going through the same experience, sticking it out and putting in the effort instead of opting out. It wasn't easy but we had a breakthrough and the negativity stopped, which I had thought wasn't possible to change as it seemed to be her mindset.

Heath: One of the remaining things my wife said to me before we ended our marriage was that I had always put my work first, my friends and family second leaving her behind in third place. In the aftermath of the divorce, I reflected on this and felt hurt that she hadn't called this out before so that I may have done something about it. I let my bitterness get the better of me and refused to pay her half of my money. It was to take me many years to really 'get' what my wife had truly meant by third best or last, as I'm now sure it must have felt to her. I did finally GET IT, but it came at a huge cost to my business and health. I was lying in a hospital bed with no money, my business in tatters with my family interstate and no partner around me while the man in the bed next to me had a steady stream of family and friends bringing food, love and laughter on a daily basis. Yeah, I GOT it. But there were so many signs before that one, all of which I let my character convince me it wasn't a lesson for me. One particularly poignant sign came through a woman called Cassie who I had been introduced to. I found her attractive, and I was trying to work out the sign of this since not only did she look like my ex-wife but she also had the same name. I pursued my interest in Cassie by introducing her to a woman in my hometown that I thought would benefit her research. At this meeting, I spotted my ex-wife in the distance. I hadn't seen her for 8 years and the last encounter had been in court. I was reeling at the sight of her, but I'd just been in a romantic situation where I felt the brunt of rejection and being treated 'last' so I felt like I'd learnt a lesson and could see how my ex-wife had felt. I approached her and we had a civil chat about the coincidence of bumping into each other and swapped stories of our families. I didn't enquire about her new partner and kids but I could see how family life had altered her appearance. She looked tired, older... like a mum, I guess. I let my ego wonder at what she must have felt watching me walk off with a younger, fitter version of herself, while she was bogged down in a relationship that possibly might have had the same problems. No doubt she actually thought *dickhead*—a label I now realise I deserved. I went on to discuss the encounter with new Cassie and its meaning, and I probably even mentioned my observations on the similarities between them both and how my ex-wife didn't look like she was having a happy life. I must have told Cassie my heroic realisation of how my recent romantic rejection had made me see the light from my ex's perspective because Cassie threw that back at me at the end of our courtship, while she also told me that *she* understood what my ex-wife had actually meant. I went on to date other women, who I would invest money in entertaining but never anything else. Leanne called me on this and told me I was conning these women with money and travel but never giving them more, when it was obvious that they were looking for a relationship. I took a break from dating because my new business venture was hitting more and more red tape—something I had no control over—and I needed to focus on it. My health also started to suffer and got progressively worse until I found myself in a hospital bed, in a different state to the one my family was in, with no-one by my side to offer me support. I wish I had put my ego aside and read the signs earlier so it didn't have to get that bad for me to wake up to myself.

The signs are there, if you look for them

Pay attention to your senses, signs, symbols, numbers, re-occurring situations, symptoms in your body, etc. These are some of the ways that Source brings your attention to something you need to understand. Have you ever found yourself wondering why you seem to attract certain situations? Do they all come at one time, in a cluster? This is one of the ways Source communicates with you to make you realise that your body is having a negative reaction to a person or situation. If you're not paying attention, Source needs to use repetition or something massive to get your attention.

Say you carry anger in your body that you inherited from your ancestry; Source would bring different types of situations that all tested your patience to activate your anger. This is Source's way of baiting your emotions, as if to say, 'Look at your reaction; it's not yours—it's a dysfunctional emotion and is causing you problems, push it out and heal.'

These are all lessons that will teach you about yourself and the world you live in. They might happen quickly—where you'll learn your lesson in one week, heal it and then move on. Other lessons can take longer, like Zac, Katherine's and Lucy's core issues, happening subtly over weeks or years. It really depends on what's in your individual body and how quickly you trust your intuition.

Don't be like Phil...

If that all seems too long and too hard, and you just read it and thought, *why bother, there's always going to be problems* then all I can tell you is that **learning is the only real purpose for your life**. Phil in *Groundhog Day* took a long time to get it; don't be like Phil. He gave up but then he had to do it over again and again—which you will too. Treat it like a game, instead of a make-or-break situation—it makes it a lot easier to persevere, especially when you get to the breakthroughs.

Emma wrote her friendship story for me a few years ago, and when I watched recently how masterfully she handled another difficult friend, I asked her to revisit the story with her new understanding. She was amazed to see the difference in her perspective—even though in her original version, she recognised Liz's purpose in her life, she still thought Liz's negativity was at fault. It was only after years of healing that she had the wisdom to handle a difficult friend differently. Instead of the anger and frustration she had used with Liz, she used patience and love and the outcome was completely different. It shone the light on the friend, who in turn realised her own negativity and she could heal her emotion and turn her perspective around to a positive one. This is an excellent example of how working on yourself can have an effect on those around you.

Ask yourself questions

Learn the language of Source by analysing everything that happens to you, literally every single thing in your life. But do this lightly, in a detached way. Don't dwell on it and add emotional pain. The best way to do this is to take a step back and examine it from all angles and ask lots of questions like:

- How did the situation/person make me feel?
- Why do I react like that?
- Why did I react by getting defensive?
- Is it the other's person's fault?
- Why are they acting that way?
- Could I have done something different?
- Why did they say that to me?

- Did that wisdom come from that person's character or Source?

Keep asking yourself questions, stepping into the shoes of each person involved, until the answer comes to you. If you can't find the answer, sit with it—but don't dwell on it—and Source will bring you more information when the time is right. This will help you see your life with a fifth-dimension perspective, in an open-minded way, allowing you to see it for what it is—an inherited emotion that doesn't belong to you—so you don't need to take on the blame, instead simply catch the emotion and heal it. This is the best way for you to make amends for your inherited dysfunction and how it caused you to react and inflict pain on others. Healing your body of dysfunctional emotions will help you come to trust Source and your intuition more and more. Trust in the signs, they're there to help you.

Chapter 5

All your relationships are a reflection of you

In the third dimension, you label the people in your life depending on their level of importance to you, as well as how long you have known them. Those who are close in relationship are 'mother', 'father', 'husband', 'wife', 'child', 'friend', and so on to the not-so close, like 'doctor', 'acquaintance', 'shop assistant' and 'stranger'. Problems arise in the third dimension when you form an emotional attachment, or expectation, as to how a person you labelled as 'important' should treat you. You assume they should treat you well because you gave them a high-value label—yet they don't always meet your expectations.

Zac's story back in Chapter 3 is a good example of how we can attribute labels to the people in our lives with expectations that can cause us to form an emotional attachment. If you recall, Zac's core issue was self-worth that had him continuously change his work life in an attempt to finally win his parents' elusive approval. What you might not recall from his story was that his marriage failure came about because of his wife's infidelity. During that time he hit rock bottom emotionally and was in a dark place as he navigated his way through the breakdown of his marriage. His parents were unsupportive of the split and he wasn't to know that their marriage had gone through the exact same infidelity issue and they had remained together. Rather than provide support without judgement, Zac's parents verbalised their own dysfunctions to reinforce the decisions they had made in their own marriage.

There is a purpose to your relationships

There's really nothing wrong with giving labels and having expectations, just as long as you give them to the people who have earned them. Look at your parents as just people, without any family attachment and no 'Mum' or 'Dad' label. Imagine they are strangers on the street that you are observing from a distance. Look at how they behave. Do they deserve the label 'Mum' and 'Dad'? Sit with this idea for a moment and look at every person in your life in the same way. Take away all their labels, so they're just human beings. Can you now see how the label comes with an emotional attachment?

When you come into the fifth-dimension way of

thinking, you realise it's not the label that's important. Your father could be a person you wouldn't associate with if it weren't for the label 'father'. When you really look at it, you see that everyone can be a parent—yet how many people actually earn the right to be called 'father' or 'mother'? If someone isn't earning the high-value label of 'mother', 'father', or whatever label you've given them, you should remove your emotional attachment to that label. Now try to flip it around on yourself and ask; *have I really earned the labels the people in my life have given me?*

What does your relationship say about you? Do you know how many people complain about their relationships? More often than not, these complaints just focus on what the other person is doing wrong. I've done it myself. I still catch myself doing it, so I know it's not easy to look at the role you play in a relationship. But no matter what stage you are at with your healing, there is a purpose for every person in your life. Be aware that the way you view your relationships—and their degree of importance to you—changes as you move from the third dimension into the fifth.

Remember, everyone fits in your life and

everyone has a purpose in either of the dimensions. To break this down, use a piece of paper and list all the people you know. Write down all your friends, right down to your acquaintances. Now, divide them into two categories: three-dimensional and fifth-dimensional. Who would you put where?

Think of how they fit in; either they're third dimension—someone you just have a chit-chat with over a drink; or they're fifth dimension—someone who you don't see too often but when you do, you have deeper conversations.

Doing this will help you understand the relationships in your life and make you wiser in your choices when it comes to seeking out the right people to talk to. If you recall the different dimension stages, you can see how people are stuck in these stages. So, third-dimension relationships are surface level and generally concern chit-chat about your day-to-day experiences. Fifth-dimension relationships have more depth and are usually about bigger concerns in your life. Both of these relationship options are important in your life. Sometimes your healing will be difficult and you may need to talk about it deeply with an open-minded, fifth-dimension friend. Other times a difficulty could create a desire to put it aside for a while and for that a third-dimension friend who will talk lightly with you and not get into things too deeply is perfect. Both styles of friendship have a place in your life and your healing experience.

How emotional scars can haunt your present

Emotional trauma inherited through DNA is not the only negative contender in your emotional vibration, this can also come about through life events that cause a scar or wound, which will act like a red flag when a similar event occurs. These emotional scars act in the same way inherited ancestry emotional pain does—the difference is they are easy to pinpoint their origin in your early life.

In Zac's marriage breakdown and at the beginning of his subsequent relationship with his current wife, Lisa, his scar presented itself straightaway. He voiced this to Lisa, saying; 'What's the point if it leads to the same outcome?' Lisa highlighted his scar to him by asking if she was behaving in a similar fashion to his ex-wife and, if not, why he would expect the same outcome. This was enough for Zac to realise his scar came from his past experience and was enough to snap him out of giving up on the relationship.

Although this effectively healed Zac's scar, both he and Lisa went through a turbulent start to their relationship, which resulted in Lisa forming an emotional wound, which was later activated in a dispute with their neighbours. It was shortly after his first marriage broke down and Zac officially split from his ex-wife, when he met Lisa. At the beginning, and noting Zac's parents opposition to their relationship, Lisa insisted Zac go back to his ex and try to make it work, telling him she didn't want him to use their fling as a get-out clause. Lisa knew if they built a relationship on anything less than a solid foundation, there would be consequences later on. When Zac discovered his ex-wife was pregnant to the man she was having an affair with, he knew there was nothing to salvage.

Despite all this, Zac's parents let it be known that they disagreed with his new relationship and that he should return to his marriage. Zac's a little different to Lisa in that he's comfortable talking about his emotions, while Lisa isn't comfortable with her emotions. During the course of their relationship,

Zac's influence rubbed off on Lisa so her defence mechanism switched from numbing her emotions to attacking. When their neighbours took a dispute over a boundary line to the tribunal, it didn't affect Zac because he knew the by-law would result in their favour and if it didn't, there were always negotiating options about its impact on the building. He could easily compartmentalise the effect and was able to chat away to his neighbours without it affecting his life. Lisa on the other hand was consumed by rage over the injustice of it. She had trouble walking past her neighbours when she wanted to shout and scream at them.

If you are the one who is reacting, then you need to find the origin of the emotion and heal it. The person—neighbour, colleague, friend—who set you off is just the bait to hook the emotion so you can pull it out. If Lisa questioned; *why am I reacting? Why am I in a rage over how unfair it is? Where have I felt this before? In my childhood?* and located the original emotion, then she can set about healing it.

Goodbye: healing (non-ancestry) emotional scars

Tip: It might help to speak this next passage aloud and record your voice, then play it back as you do the healing allowing your voice to guide you as you concentrate on the visualisations—just as my voice would guide you in my clinic.

[START]
- Come into your heart.
- Feel your heart.
- Stay in your heart as you do the healing.
- Now, recall the emotion overpowering your body. Bait it again if you have to.
- Feel the emotion, but don't take it on.
- Go back to the child and situation, as if you are there. Lock in the memory with your mind's eye, not your logical head.
- Now play it out—visualise yourself as the child in the situation.
- Bring the healer you are today into the situation to advise your child self how to take back their strength.
- Think of what wisdom you would advise a child in your life and say this to your child self.

- Let your body guide you through it.
- Your healer self may want to advise a tough approach, such as telling the person loudly and clearly that their behaviour is not acceptable!
- If your child mind's eye is telling you that the perpetrator of the painful emotion is not listening—then look at them without the label and throw them in the bin/pit and take your strength back.
- As the healer, take the hand of your child self and tell the child that it's going to be all right.
- If the child is not responding or can't let go and wants to hold on to the resentment out of revenge, send the child into the sky.
- Allow the essence of your soul to step out of your body and throw the character you are and your child self away into the sky.
- Visualise the emotion going into the sky with the child.
- Feel it leaving your body forever.
- Now come back into your body, into your heart and allow your soul to break out of this broken body.
- Let your soul come above your body and rise up into the heavens and allow Source/God to nourish your soul and give you strength, compassion, wisdom, patience, abundance and joy.
- Take these tools and allow these tools to nourish

your soul.
- Thanking Source/God, come back down to earth, walk through a tunnel, walk to the end of this tunnel.
- Let go.
- Visualise a white door at the end of the tunnel.
- Open it and step into your new body—letting go of the past.
- See yourself in 5, 10, 20 years' time and so on... just enjoy letting go.

[END]

The magnetic effect in your relationships

Every person you attract into your life can be there for the purpose of bringing out the worst in you. This is actually a blessing because they will awaken you to your own dysfunctions. If you're not aware of this, rather than examine the emotion and see how it relates to you, you might just think a person is 'toxic' and push them out of your life. Doing this serves you no purpose because **you need to activate dysfunctional emotions in order to push them out**. Keep in mind that there is a reason for every person in your life, including those people you can't get away from—like work colleagues! Heal the emotions as they rise—pushing them back down won't work, as you'll just keep attracting the same people or situations, again and again, until you learn to heal the emotion they bring up in you.

Your life has an emotional pattern

Use the mapping tool to get the full picture of the patterns and rhythms of your emotional life. A map of your entire life, from pre-birth to right now, including your family's lives, will signpost the emotions that are inherited, and the ones that are scars from your childhood or early life. Think of mapping as your chance to rewind and really find out who you are—the payoff will be an easier recognition of the emotions when you do your healing.

Start with a timeline of your life

Using pencil and paper (do not use a pen or a computer as these will not allow you to access your subconscious mind), make a timeline from the day you were born, noting every age to the age you are now, leaving room to add in notes. Using the information you have already gathered about your family over the years, note down details about your birth, such as the position you were born into, your family's culture, status, socio demographic, financial status, etc. If you don't know this information, ask your family for it. If you're adopted, or you can't access your ancestry information, you can still find out about you by mapping your life with your new family. Carry on working through each age. What happened to you at 2, 3, 4, 5... 15, 16, 17... 25, 26, 27... 35, 36, 37... and so on.

Jot down events that happened to you at every age, no matter how insignificant they may seem. What have you heard about yourself at these ages? Was there any trauma? Think about times where your life has been interrupted. Maybe a parent left, or a relative died? See if these events have had an effect on you in your 20s and 30s. Do you still get stuck with that emotion? For example, do you still feel the same loneliness you did since your first love/parents/guardian left when you were a particular age?

Look at your life for patterns in relationships, friendships, partnerships, illnesses, stresses, finances—everything and anything that's had an effect or caused you emotional pain.

Now make a timeline for your family

When you've done the map of your life, do one for each family member. Become an investigative journalist of your family's story and hound every member; annoy them if you have to... just keep asking until you get the full picture of your family—as far back as you can go. Ask your family what they know or remember hearing about your ancestors' lives. Include your siblings, parents and grandparents—jot down what you know about them and their patterns.

Find the patterns

When you've mapped everyone's lives you can start to see patterns emerge. Look at your map and see the patterns of people and situations that you have attracted into your life:

- Do you continually attract the same drama into your life, no matter how many times you try and change your circumstances?
- Do you and your spouse have similar family histories? For example:
- Have either of your sets of parents split up because of death or divorce?

- Are both of your fathers alcoholics?
- Are you both the black sheep in your families?

Look for similarities in the partners you have been attracted to:

- What common traits did they/do they have?
- Look at how your relationships have been from one to the other.
- Detail each one of all the good and bad points.
- Why did it end?
- What are the differences between the people in your relationships?
- How many loves/relationships have you had?
- Is there a habit there?
- How were they? Easy? Or dramatic and complicated?
- See if it's a family emotion by comparing the map of your life with the members in your family's lives.
- Do your siblings attract the same problems with their partners?
- What are your parents' lives together like?

- Are you acting out the same dysfunctions they had with your own partner?
- Did your father/mother have many relationships?
- What were they like? Compare your father/mother's relationships with your own.

Mapping your relationships will help you understand the source of the negative vibration in your life. **The same dysfunction in you is attracted to the same dysfunction in another person, like a magnet**, so recognising a pattern in the people you attract into your life is like holding a mirror up to your own emotional dysfunction.

Try another pattern—like money

- Did you have enough money growing up? If not, how has this affected your life?
- Maybe there was plenty of money—think: how has this affected your relationship with money now?
- Does one of your parents earn the most money? Do they share it freely with the other parent?
- Are they generous or tight with each other?

With you?

- Are you good with money? Or do you and your siblings have trouble with money?
- If you don't have the same pattern as your parents and siblings with money, where in your life did this issue first occur?
- Measure how you treat money—are you careless with it? Do you take it for granted?
- Do you use money to buy things to compensate for other problems in your life?
- Does money fuel your addictions?
- Does your partner do any of these things?

Mapping a family pattern: example money issues

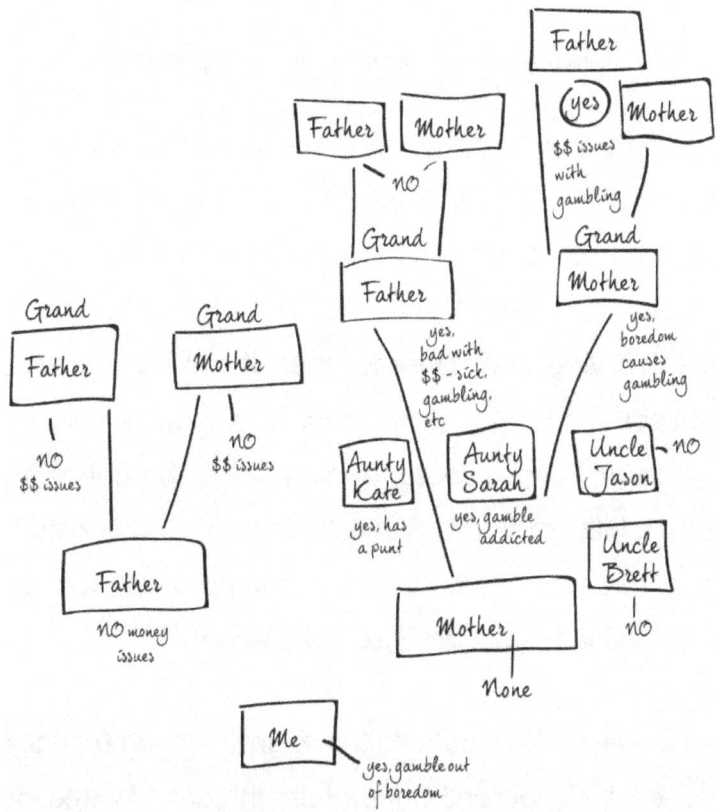

As you are mapping, narrow the emotions down into those you know are inherited from your DNA (this means you can't pinpoint the origin of the issue in your early life, it's as if it has always existed) and those that were created in your early life (meaning you can locate the origin of the issue in your early life and it doesn't exist for others in your family, unless they were also exposed to it).

Was your childhood interrupted?

How peaceful, comforting and stable was your childhood? Every child deserves to enjoy a carefree and loving childhood. Family life should be focused on the child's quality of life, *not their parents*. If yours wasn't loving and carefree, then it will have had a consequence on your emotional life. Abuse, divorce and death all contribute to interrupting the normality and stability of your childhood home life. This would have caused you emotional trauma, which will be contributing to your emotional vibration.

0–12 years old: The result of an interruption (usually caused by a parent's departure through divorce or death) this early would create neediness in you towards one of your parents. You would have been apprehensive, which then becomes a sense of 'doom' in adulthood that your partner will eventually leave you, too. Remember, your child's mind lacks adult logic so it recorded the emotional trauma of your parent leaving in your subconscious mind as: *'people who love me leave me'*. Then, as an adult, in your intimate relationships the recording *'people who love me leave me'* plays in the back of your mind on repeat, creating that intense insecurity that the partner you love will leave you like your parent did. In some cases, this feeling of doom can be so intense that the adult-logical mind will rationalise that these feelings are too overpowering and it's just easier to be alone, or you will drive your partner away with your neediness and insecurity—so that *'people who love me leave me'* then becomes a self-fulfilling prophecy.

13–17 years old: An interruption during puberty activates an 'attack' defence mechanism, causing you to rebel against the parent who stayed. This means you end up hating both parents as a result of your emotional turmoil, leaving you feeling isolated and hot-tempered with no-one to turn to. A child who feels this way quickly learns techniques to shut down their emotions and block out the pain. Then, as an adult, you can attract a weaker partner who you verbally attack when the early trauma is activated. This can mean a rebellious girl can turn into a woman who fights with her husband, while a rebellious boy can turn into a man who uses drugs or alcohol to repress his aggression. The teenager who takes on the responsibility of filling in for the absent parent by taking care of the remaining parent and their siblings, or who overcompensates to become the best teenager, can become an adult victim to a dominating or controlling partner.

What character do you play?

Recognising the character you play in this life will help you to acknowledge your dysfunctional reactions to circumstances you come across so that you can separate them. Start by looking inwards—pretend you're an observer watching someone else. Now, imagine your life is a soap opera and think about the character you play in the drama:

- DRAMA QUEEN You have BIG reactions (more like OVERreaction) to every little thing...
- WILD CHILD You are flighty and just can't seem to focus or settle, there's always something better around the corner...

- VINDICTIVE People are just plain nasty and always out to get you...
- MARTYR You love to fix people or take up a cause to feel important...
- ATTENTION SEEKER It's always about you, even when it isn't...
- WISE ONE You know more than most, and love to dispense advice wherever you go...

Identify a character and how it fits into your life. The character that resonates with you, annoys or grates on you is most likely the one that you are playing in your life. This is your default reaction to situations in your life. Remember this so that you can be open-minded about the part you play in the situations that come up in your life. This will help you to **detach from reacting emotionally and allow you to look at a situation for what it is—an opportunity to learn a lesson** about yourself and heal a negative emotion that serves your life no purpose.

Chapter 6

The evolution of you

As you evolve from the version of you that was at the mercy of your emotions into the new you, there will be different challenges at each stage. **To master the game of your life, healing needs to be a daily habit** so that you don't fall back into your old third-dimensional way of thinking. As you develop your daily routine of checking in with your emotional state, knowing that your emotions are being baited to show you an important lesson about *you*, you will naturally find the tools that work best for you.

Find tools that work for you

Getting through some of the rougher bumps on your healing road will require you having plenty of tools to help you avoid your breakthroughs turning into break*downs*.

Sitting with an emotion: The most effective healing comes when the emotion has hit its peak, and this can happen naturally if you let it. You can learn a lot by letting a situation in your life come to its natural peak. If it's not overpowering your body, sit with it—as in let it rest and see what happens. Healing isn't a fast-track to a perfect life, it takes time to work through the levels and that happens differently for everyone. If you are not overwhelmed by the emotion, sit with it and see how it unfolds. Source/God has an amazing ability to help you bring up the emotion and play it out when it's the right time. In this way, life events can be their own healing session. When you can distance yourself from the emotion, map it back to its origin and let yourself understand the role you play in attracting drama and dysfunction.

Writing tool: Putting pencil to paper and writing out your emotions can quieten your conscious mind from using its logical reasoning, allowing your subconscious mind to come forward and express itself. And there are plenty of ways pencil and paper can be effective:

- Your subconscious mind is full of painful memories of times when you didn't speak up for yourself or address an issue. Writing these emotions out allows you to go back to that situation and that person—so that you can deactivate the memory and re-write your own emotional history.

- When an emotion is overpowering you, like anger, writing everything and anything that pops into your head to do with that emotion helps reduce the force of it in your body, so you can distance yourself from it. This will help you get behind the emotion and push it out in a healing session.
- Addressing a letter to someone you have a problem with in your life can give you the space to see the issue from both perspectives—the recipient of the letter and yours. Even though you know you'll never send it, the act of writing tricks your subconscious into believing the letter will be sent and allows you to see it from the recipient's point of view.
- You can use writing as a way of talking to Source/God and asking for guidance.

Grab a pencil and paper; then read this carefully: First feel the emotion, bait it if you have to. Now address the letter to the person you had/have the issue with, scribbling down whatever pops into your head. *It's important that you don't re-read as you write out a dysfunctional emotion.* If you do, your body will just take it all back on again. Dump every thought, emotion and feeling down about the situation or person. Don't worry if it looks like one big scribble, no-one is going to read it. For a chronic emotion that's overpowering your body—write as frenzied as you feel. You can swear and say what you like, whatever it takes to get every detail of the emotion out of your body. When you've finished writing your letter, and all the emotion is out of your body, burn the pages—or rip them up and flush them down the toilet—and visualise the emotion and hurt is disappearing into ash or being washed away.

First aid: As you evolve, it's possible that an activation of one emotion can ricochet and feel chronic or catastrophic—very like depression, anxiety, panic or fear. It's BIG, and it will take over your whole body. This will feel incredibly painful, forcing you to numb yourself to cope. Emotional dysfunction is a magnet for similar dysfunctions, which can set off a cluster of associated dysfunctions in you to create an overwhelming emotional feeling. It might feel like an overpowering sense of 'Why me?' and result in you throwing yourself a self-pity party. When this happens, you need an emergency 'first aid kit'. Whatever works for you! Call a friend or family member to talk—not necessarily about your problems but do something together to distract you from your thoughts. Don't be alone, as you will just risk feeding into the negativity. It might be that your body is not able to cope with the truth, so the best you can do is push it aside *for now* and do something, anything, not to dwell in it. Dwelling will only feed the negativity and make it worse.

There is a reason for what's happening to you

Healing can be incredibly tough. It's rewarding when you get through it, but the lesson is painful while it happens. All I can tell you is, just keep going—you will get through it. **Don't run away, it will only get worse. Just know that whatever situation you are in is just for now.** It's easy to wallow in misery but before you give up and sink into the depths of despair, find out if there is anything you can do first. Maybe you are struggling to have a baby; have you exhausted all options—adoption, fostering, egg donors, sperm donors, and surrogacy? If you're still single but miserable about it; see what you can actually do about it. If you're going from work to home and not actually getting out of your circle of friends, are you really expecting anything to change? There's plenty of dating resources now, find the one that works for you and let it lead to your partner. If you're struggling with finances, get honest with yourself. Ditch the fun stuff, the paid lunches, the triple-a-day coffees and seek help—live with your parents if you have to.

There is always hope. If you're not on the path you think you should be on, maybe that's because Source/God is talking to you and taking you to another path that you need to be on. Unless there is a healing, sometimes you just have to surrender to your life and know that the purpose of your suffering will reveal itself in time.

With wisdom comes great responsibility

Now that your intuition has strengthened, you will find yourself speaking and seeking the truth with compassion for humanity. Your newfound empathy for fellow sufferers is natural to you, with the understanding that not everyone has access to his or her truth. When you learn to step into somebody else's shoes, you experience life from their point of view, rather than from just your own perspective—allowing you to remove all judgement, criticism and opinion that used to be a part of your thinking.

The advantage of seeing a situation from all points of view means it's tempting to excuse dysfunctional behaviour by the people you love or admire because you understand the motivation behind it. Don't. **It's not up to you to shelter another person from feeling their emotions—it's how they will learn their lessons.** No matter what, you are responsible for your behaviour and that means not excusing anyone's bad behaviour.

You don't need to get into a fight, just explain that it's not okay with love, compassion and empathy (not talking down to the person or provoking them) as if they were your child. You don't need to hurt others with words, but nor do you need to hurt yourself by not speaking your truth if someone is hurting you. You also don't need to devalue your truth by altering your behaviour and thoughts to fit in with someone else's idea of who you are.

There are no excuses for bad behaviour

Trying to be a good person can sometimes lead to excusing bad behaviour in others. While your intention is good, or you are trying to avoid conflict, the outcome has consequences for you and the person whose behaviour you are excusing.

My client Sandra is a soft, gentle woman who came from a middle-class suburban family. She married and had two boys, John and Paul, but struggled with her husband's lack of parenting and financial responsibility. Many years later, she decided her boys would be better off without her husband so she asked for a divorce. Coping with the divorce and life as a single mother was difficult and Sandra often felt depressed, which also had an effect on her children. John reacted to his father's absence and Sandra's depression by becoming rebellious. Sandra didn't know how to handle this erratic behaviour, so rather than fight him she let him have more freedom. Her youngest son, Paul, reacted to the chaos in his home life, and fear of losing another parent, by taking on the responsibilities of his absent father. John's rebellion meant he stayed out more and more to avoid seeing his mother depressed. To fill the void left by his family break-up, he ended up in a well-known gang that made him feel part of a 'brotherhood'. Shortly after, he got a girl pregnant. He wasn't a responsible father, because he was more interested in the gang but they were only using John to sell their drugs. John ended up getting caught and was given a suitable prison sentence for selling drugs. Feeling sorry for him, Sandra regularly visits and brings along her young grandson to visit his father. Paul's life has been a lot softer than John's, but he has never found a relationship. Sandra has since remarried. When she came to see me, Sandra didn't know what to do about John's situation, but was grateful that she didn't have to worry about Paul.

Sandra's story has quite a few incidents of excusing another person's bad behaviour that has consequences for a number of people involved.

- Taking away his 'son' label, John was selling drugs to people and Sandra knew about it and did nothing. By not confronting her son about his moods and illegal activities, Sandra was excusing his behaviour—if you recall my story in the first chapter of this book, drugs come with a karmic consequence. Sandra saying nothing is excusing the behaviour.

- By bringing her grandchild to visit, Sandra is not only normalising prison in the impressionable eyes of a young child, but she is again excusing the fact that bad behaviour has a disastrous consequence by rewarding him with time with his son.
- By cushioning him from the consequences of his behaviour, Sandra is preventing John from learning his lesson. He knows no matter how bad it gets, his mother will look after his child and support him financially. Sandra's actions are getting in the way of John hitting rock bottom, where he would get the opportunity to reflect on his life and understand how his dysfunctions had lead him to prison. **Saving someone from feeling emotional pain, can actually prevent that person from realising their mistakes and having the opportunity to make positive changes in their life.**
- If he had chosen the right road, John would have more wisdom and empathy for his own son and would have corrected his actions before they led him to prison. John should know that his absence will hurt his child's life, as his was hurt by his father's absence.
- Paul's dysfunction is not as obvious as John's because he leads a quieter life, meaning his issues go under the radar. As a child, taking over the role of

'man of the house' meant Paul had to grow up emotionally quicker than other boys his age. Paul believes his lack of a relationship is due to the fact that he hasn't found the right woman. He doesn't realise that his subconscious mind thinks all relationships are like his parents and end the same way, so he doesn't open himself up to meeting the right woman.

When I made these points to Sandra and told her that she was the one that needed to make the changes that would lead to a better outcome for her children, she stopped bringing her grandson to prison and while supportive emotionally, she began letting her children take responsibility for themselves. Shortly after his release from prison, John's girlfriend overdosed and died. As much as she wanted to, Sandra didn't intervene. She watched on as John found and maintained a reliable job, took full custody of his son and became a responsible parent.

Your choices have consequences

From the day you are born, you are bombarded with messages telling you how you can live the 'perfect life'. This message comes at you through advertising, TV shows and media imagery. It's a constant stream of visual messages that tell you what perfect looks like: body, style, home, car, intelligence, friendship, love, relationships, marriage, parenting, wealth and health. It's impossible to reach perfection, and it can create a misery in you that makes you turn to 'reward-like' items to numb your pain. I've seen plenty of people who are bored, restless, or in an emotional upheaval do it. While the immediate gratification helps, over the long-term it inevitably adds its own kind of pain. Most substances have an addictive element to them because they bring you pleasure, so be careful.

The real cost of rewarding yourself

'Busy' wasn't a concept in your grandparents' life, and probably not too much of your parents. In today's world, busy has taken on a whole new level of meaning. There is little downtime, we are constantly switched to on—racing from home to work, work to social activities—for ourselves, our kids—to home and bed; all the while we are contactable through our phones for both work and socialising. We hardly have time to unwind before we have to hit the ground running again. Even if we schedule our lives to the last minute, something will happen to throw us out of whack and then the whole balance comes undone. This level of busyness and stress is causing many of us to 'reward' ourselves with alcohol or something similar for getting through a tough day or situation—this is fine in moderation but they can easily become habits that can develop into their own problems. Rewards are also being used as a form of escapism to numb ourselves from the misery we feel at having a less than perfect life. There are many ways to numb your emotions: alcohol, drugs, food, shopping, gambling, sex, and gadgets are just a few of these. You might use these things for pleasure. But how many times have you used them as a reward for getting through a tough time? How many times have you overused them to numb yourself from feeling emotional pain?

Get real with yourself:
- How many times have you stayed out partying because you don't want to go home alone?
- How many times have you used alcohol or drugs to numb your emotional pain?

- How many times have you used sex to feel loved?
- How often do you eat to fill a void?
- How many times have you annoyed someone else with unnecessary arguments and fights, rather than look inwards at your own problems?

When something changes from being a reward, to a quick fix, then to *needing* it to get through every day, it's no longer fixing anything, and is creating more dysfunctions and problems in your life.

The answer isn't at the end of a bottle

Once it was socially acceptable to consume alcohol to celebrate at a party, now it's become medicinal as a cure for getting through a particularly hard day at work or a gruelling parenting day. Do you recall your parent or grandparent turning to wine? I'm sure they wanted to but it's highly likely that doing so was deemed alcoholic behaviour. Rewarding yourself with alcohol after everyday activities, like work and childrearing, can easily become a habit that you depend on to unwind. Then the quantity of drinks spirals out of control—one glass turns into two, three and so on. Before you know it, you're hooked and need a drink, or several, every day to unwind. Using alcohol in this way is dangerous, because it removes your self-control and alters your thoughts and poisons your ability to see your life with a fifth-dimension point of view. Too much alcohol and you stop thinking logically and rationally, which will inevitably create havoc in your life.

If you're not forming a habit in your everyday life, you might feel the need to use alcohol in social situations to give you a boost or help your confidence. Alcohol has the ability to change your personality to help you overcome being shy and awkward so that you are confident enough to talk to anyone. Instead of understanding or accepting shyness or social awkwardness, you cover it with alcohol to get you through. This is just another slippery slope. First you need it to improve your social skills at the odd occasion, but before long you need it at all social gatherings. Soon you need it to get through every day. Instead of trying to understand your emotions and why certain things are difficult, you're drowning them in alcohol.

Get real with yourself:

- How many times have you used alcohol to cover your emotions, only to totally lose control of your behaviour?
- Have you ever woken up and not known what's happened the night before?
- Have you had to piece together your behaviour based on other people's interpretations?
- How many times have you excused your behaviour and others because you were *just drunk*?

Some people can enjoy alcohol occasionally without an effect—moderation means you can take it or leave it, you don't need to have it. If you have answered yes to even one of the above questions, then you are at risk when you touch alcohol. It has the potential to alter your thoughts and behaviour, putting you in danger with serious consequences to your life.

Warning: Your alcohol tolerance will lower as you remove your dysfunctional emotions and you become more in-tune with your body.

Drugs don't work

Marijuana, speed, cocaine, ecstasy, heroin, ice, hallucinogens etc., are highly addictive substances that have the ability to severely alter your thoughts and behaviour. They are very powerful and it's for good reason that they are illegal. When you first use these drugs, the initial reaction in your body is positive. It brings confidence and euphoria, lifting your mood. Suddenly your life is problem-free and you can handle anything that comes your way. This high lasts so briefly and is always followed by a crashing low. At first the downer is about as manageable as an alcohol hangover. You might even reason that it is a small price to pay for such an amazing euphoria. A one-day recovery period starts to extend to a few days of mild depression.

Soon you need more and more drugs to offset the downer. When you're high, you're open to negative energy, which means that when you come out of the high, you feel depressed and can only see the negative in everyone and everything. To feel good again, you need to get high, but this soon creates a vicious circle of getting high, taking on negative energy, followed by crashing lows and needing to get high again to feel good. Before you know it, you're in an addictive spiral and you no longer have any control of whether you want to get high or not, now you *need* to get high to function.

There are many health issues that come from using drugs, including paranoia and depression. With prolonged use, taking drugs can lead to serious mental health issues and even death. Jack in Chapter One carried karma with him from selling drugs and John, Sandra's son, in this Chapter ended up in prison. I know even more people who have overdosed and died. The only way to prevent this happening to your life is to avoid all forms of illicit drugs.

Are you eating to survive or eating to compensate?

The right nutrition is essential to your survival, but when you eat excessively to fill an emotional void, it creates the same effect on your life as abusing alcohol and drugs.

Get real with yourself:

- How often do you use food as a reward rather

than fuel for your body?
- Do you say to yourself, *I've had a hard week, I'm going to have that cake to reward myself?*
- How often do you eat past the point of satisfying your hunger?
- When it comes to reward foods do you ever think, *No, that is bad for my health, so I won't have it?*
- How often can you honestly say you eat the right foods?

Much like how alcohol and drugs creates a high/low effect on your life, food addiction works in the same way. Reward eating is fine in moderation, but it gets out of control when you gorge on food past the point of satisfying your hunger. Your body can't process this excess, so it stores it as fat. Thanks to the image of the perfect body posted on every magazine, TV advert and movie, you know that the fat your body is carrying doesn't fit this perfect image. You don't stop eating because it makes you feel good, so you focus on ways to get rid of the fat. You try everything: going to the gym, fad diets, every way you can think of to get the fat off. But food is your friend, your reward, so you constantly return to eating.

If food isn't a reward, you might see it as the enemy and punish yourself by only eating the bare minimum. It's easier to focus on food as friend or enemy, rather than look inwards at your misery. Comfort eating adds a layer of dysfunction to your life. If you're struggling with overeating, seek guidance from support groups that can help with food addictions.

My client Susan was born two years after her older brother, who suffers from Attention Deficit Disorder (ADD). Susan was a quiet child—much to her mother's relief who was struggling with the demands of her firstborn. Susan spent most of her first year in a carrier, until it was time for a feed. When she was finished feeding, she was placed back into the carrier until the next feed. She was rarely taken out of the carrier for a cuddle or playing, as her brother had been, because her mother struggled to focus on the two children at once.

Because her only experience of nurturing and comfort was when she was held at feeding time, Susan subconsciously associated food with nurturing and love. As she grew older, Susan yearned for the comfort of food, even if she wasn't hungry. Comfort eating led to Susan gaining more weight than others girls her age, so when she started school, Susan found herself standing out as fatter than the other kids. When she was teased or pointed at, Susan's character played the victim card believing everyone was against her, which meant she continued the cycle of finding comfort in eating. She avoided most social events, and if she did go she would eat before and after rather than let anyone see how much she ate. Susan's misery wasn't just about the food, she also belittled thinner girls in her circle of friends about other things so they would just feel as bad about themselves as she did about herself. When Susan began healing it became very clear that she needed to address the eating because it was keeping her in her misery. With the help of Food Addicts Anonymous, Susan fought her misery and now no longer eats for comfort.

Let's talk about sex

As part of a healthy and loving relationship, sex has a purpose in bringing two people closer together. Even when it's not in relationship, sex can be happily enjoyed between two consenting adults—although if the boundaries are not clearly defined for sex in these circumstances, it can lead to confusion and hurt. Used excessively, and by conning another person into having sex with you, it can have the same effect as abuse of *alcohol and drugs on your life.*

Get real with yourself:

- How often do you engage in a flirtation, hoping to coerce someone into having sex with you?
- When you do manage to score at the end of a flirtation, do you want the other person to leave immediately?
- Have you ever woken up after a boozy night with someone in your bed but you don't recall how they got there?
- Do you find yourself having affairs with married people so that you get your sex hit without all the complications that comes with a single person?

Libido is a necessary function of our human body and I'm not suggesting you abstain from having sex; what you need to be careful of is your intention with it. If you're pursuing someone and are not upfront about your intentions for a casual encounter, then you're misleading that person. Of course, you're less likely to be successful if you're honest about your intentions, so it's tempting to say nothing—you could probably reason that this absolves you of guilt because they never asked and you didn't lie. You're wrong. Knowing someone cares for you and wants more than sex means you are engaging in sex with the wrong intention. Pursuing a person who is married or in a relationship with someone else is also wrong and it will hurt people.

Using your influence to create a situation with the wrong intention, so that you can have sex with another person, comes with the same highs and lows that food, alcohol and drug users feel. A euphoric high when you get what you want, followed by an ultimate low that these addictions are preventing you from fulfilling some of your life goals. All of these things, when abused, add problems to your life. Seek help with this problem; there are plenty of support groups.

My client Greg's father is a passionate soccer fan and of the larrikin boys' culture that surrounds it; which rubbed off onto Greg. His mother was the opposite and was interested in spirituality, which also had an effect on Greg, but often the lad culture in him won out. When a colleague mentioned my work to Greg, he was curious about the spirituality, so he sought me out for a reading. I could see how his parents' DNA was causing a divide in Greg's life. He was 35 years old and very much wanted to settle down, but said he couldn't find the right woman. He was active in soccer, loved drinking with the boys and was popular with women. As we worked on healing his emotions, it became apparent that Greg was using sex with the wrong intentions. Women found him very attractive and charismatic and he had plenty of opportunities with the right women, but after he had been intimate with a woman he immediately wanted her to leave and had no desire to see her again. Greg reasoned that he hadn't mislead any women because he had never made them promises, yet I could tell these women had false hope that something would come of it. I explained to him that he needed to be upfront about his intentions or it was misleading. Drinking alcohol didn't help; as he often found himself waking up in the morning next to a woman and wasn't sure how she had got there. But even then, when the alcohol had worn off he had no remorse and just wanted them gone. He even turned to married women who were prone to cheating, reasoning that he wasn't harming single women by fulfilling his desires with this type of woman. I explained that this had karmic consequences for his future relationship and that it was morally wrong. Greg's ego enjoyed the power that he could get any woman he wanted, and sex came with a feeling of euphoria that was attractive to him, but the fact he couldn't even lie next to his sexual partner afterwards was preventing him from finding a woman he could marry and have a future with. First, I advised him to cut out alcohol, so he had a clear understanding of his interactions with women when he was in a social setting. Secondly, I advised him to give his body a break from sex for a while so it would lose the memory of the euphoria. He could still date, but he could only kiss them—this way he had to focus on the person and her suitability as a life partner. The idea was that he could go beyond kissing when he'd worked out if he had the right intentions and wanted to have a relationship with her. This took Greg a long time of trial and error before he could overcome his temptations. He was eventually able to find a partner.

The power of one

Now think about how other people's choices will have an impact on your life. To give you an idea, think of when an accident happens in peak hour on the road you're driving on, or on the track your train is travelling on. Everything comes to a standstill, displacing hundreds and thousands of people from their commute. The train line gets shut down, commuters are forced to take alternative transport. Throw in bad weather and the struggle is even worse.

Your life has a similar vibration that impacts the people around you, as those lives do on yours—so your choices matter to more than just you. Now throw in social conditioning (AKA peer pressure) and life can get tougher still. On top of that, the cost of living keeps getting higher and higher, adding to all our stress levels, and that's all before we add in those extra problems that come from using substances like alcohol and drugs.

Social conditioning

The minute you enter the world, you are taught right from wrong, along with many other rules, customs and manners that help billions of us co-habit in this world. Your parents, school, work, government and many more institutions have a say in what rules you need to abide by. You quickly learn to toe the line when you realise breaking the rules can have negative consequences. Over the course of your life, you can easily fall into line with rules and regulations without thinking because you have learnt to stop questioning the need for them at all. Some rules are necessary, but the fact you've stopped questioning the need for a rule means you are easily led.

When you are easily led, you fall under the spell of social conditioning, which can subtly affect your thinking. Like peer pressure, social conditioning relies on the influence of the crowd, so that over time you gradually conform to a crowd mentality, because going against it is too hard. You might reason that *everyone's doing it, so it must be right* rather than stop and question why they, and now you, are falling into line. It's a sad truth that each of us can be lazy when it comes to finding our own answers. Rather than seeking out the truth for ourselves, we blindly follow others. We want answers now. Each of us is the master of the quick fix. We're easily sold on anything that promises us a quick fix for an issue we struggle with.

Get real with yourself:

- How many times have you done a fad diet?
- How many times have you entered a get-rich-quick scheme? Played lotto?
- How many times have you done a course that promises you happiness at the end?
- How many times have you gone to a fortune-teller to give you hope?
- How many times have you relied on doctors to tell you about your own body? (They do know a lot about the human body, but they don't exist in *your* body.)

Seek your own answers

Be a sceptic. Look beyond the label for everything. Don't swallow it automatically because a doctor, psychiatrist, politician or whoever has the 'expert' label said its fact. Use their information and find your own answer for *you*. Don't be spoon-fed by marketing and advertising labels telling you how to have the perfect life. Find out what works for you. I even encourage you to be sceptical about what you've read in this book—find out if it really works for you and your life. Be your own experiment.

Get real with yourself:
- Do you really need it?
- Why do you need it?
- Will it really give you the fix, or is it just another gimmick?
- How long have the people endorsing this product used it for?
- Will you benefit short-term or long-term?
- Is there a better investment for your problem than the time or money this quick fix is asking for?

Confront yourself; find out if you are easily led

Open your eyes and look behind the labels. Walk the aisles of a supermarket and look at it as if you had travelled through time from the 1900s. Can you recognise the food? How far removed from nature/natural is it? So now consider, is it really healthy for your body? Ask yourself what the term 'healthy' means to you. Did you come across your idea of healthy through your own research, or did you pick it up from someone else? Now really start exploring healthy for yourself—don't just swallow someone else's interpretation. Research nutrition and healthy food, and look behind the label nutrition institutions hide behind. If you do, you might actually be surprised that big food corporations who sell you junk food sponsor most nutrition institutions in Australia. Now ask yourself if their intention is to give people the best nutrition possible at an affordable price, or is to support their own funding source? Repeat this questioning in every area of your life.

Question yourself on intentions

Next time you are telling a friend, colleague or family member about a problem in your life, assess their reaction, and ask:

Get real with yourself:
- Are they quick to offer free advice?
- Do you find yourself being easily influenced by their convictions?
- What are their intentions in giving you advice?
- Who is this person offering the advice? Friend or foe?

- Does their situation reflect your own? Is that good or bad?
- What is their actual expertise? Are they in a situation that you want to be in? Are they biased?
- Are they in the same situation as you, and want you stay in it too for selfish reasons? Or are they in a better situation, but want you to stay put in yours?

These are just some of the questions you should be asking yourself when you take on free advice that is part of social conditioning. Blindly following advice without questioning the truth behind it can create problems in your life. Listen to the advice, but just question if it comes from the right intention and whether it suits *your* situation.

Maybe you find yourself asking others for advice? Stop and question why you need help making all your decisions. There really is no such thing as unbiased advice. People's advice comes from their truth, which means that it's based on their life journey, not yours, and what *they* would do in the situation you are in. Advice doesn't have to have bad intentions to have a negative effect, simply because it's their truth, not yours.

Taking on advice will lead you on their path, but then what? At the next problem, do you seek advice again? Or do you follow a completely different person's advice and get sent down another path? It's easy to see how giving up your power sets you on a journey that leads to problems in your life. We all have access to Source/God, but we are all living a different human experience. **Unless someone can experience your life, they can't make your decisions for you**.

Always examine advice very carefully, using your intuition, with the conviction that the right answer is within you. The tools in this book will help you to access your intuition and connect with Source/God so that you make the right choices for *you*. When you heal your emotional dysfunctions, you will just know what the right path is for you. I've seen it happen with my clients after many healing sessions; their wisdom is incredible.

People in your life will sense your newfound wisdom and seek you out for it. Even if they don't actively seek you out, it can be very tempting to point out to people where they are going wrong in their life, especially when you can see it from your fifth-dimension/bird's-eye view. Please tread carefully here. **When you are asked for advice, you should state very clearly that is based on your own experience** because that's all it can ever be based on.

You have free will; use it wisely

Our life in this third-dimensional world is ruled by material possessions and worth. Your thoughts can be very powerful—if you fixate on money, power, or other material possessions, it is possible for you to create the energy that will attract this into your life. But what if this is not meant for your journey in this life?

Everything in your life should be based on moderation. To will something into your life that is not for you will have consequences somewhere else. You might decide that you're going to be rich, and to do that you're going to work hard and become the CEO of a company. It's highly likely you will achieve this, but it will come at the consequence of something else. You may end up as CEO, but have no time for your relationships or anything else. When you put in the hard work to heal your emotional dysfunctions, you will notice improvements in your life. This comes with a faith that you will be guided to what is meant for you in this life.

What legacy do you want to leave behind?

Fast forward to the inevitable—your deathbed. Picture yourself lying there, reflecting on your life as it is now.

Get real with yourself:
- Do you have regrets?
- Are there things you would change?
- Who is there?
- Who do you wish was there?
- Why are they not by your side?

Nobody knows when they're going to die, but you can work on your legacy every single day from here on in. Do something today that will make sure you are surrounded by people you love when it comes time to leave this life. Change your choices—take the hard road and confront your emotions, understand them and take the steps to heal them. Putting those steps into action every day will change your vibration and have an effect on the people in your life. **You** have the power to make positive changes to your life and the lives around you.

Appendix A

Visualisation practice

... visualising with an object

- Sit with an object directly in front of you. It can be a cup, a ball or a book. Basically, just something that you can remember in detail.
- First look at the object in front of you, taking in every detail of it: its colours, angles, writing on it, and even the feeling that the object gives you.
- Now close your eyes and 'see' the object in your mind. It can be useful to alternate between closing your eyes and opening them trying to imprint the object into your vision when your eyes are closed.

... visualising an event

- Walk from your bedroom to the kitchen
- Take in every feeling of the journey; such as the pressure of your feet on the ground, smells, the outside sounds, the feeling of your bodies weight, tightness, looseness, pain and even clothes on your body. The feeling of your breath rising and falling in your chest.
- Go to the cupboard and get a cup.
- Feel its texture in your hand.

- Walk back to where you were sitting and sit down again holding the cup in your hand feeling its weight, temperature, your body against the seat.
- Put the cup down.
- Now close your eyes and replay the whole event in as much detail as you can, invoking all the feelings, sounds, etc. you experienced.

… visualising everyday habits

- Repeat the steps above with one of your habits. This can be done making a cup of tea, brushing your teeth or any activity that takes a few minutes and can be replayed in your mind. The key here is to be very present while imprinting the event.

Acknowledgements

There are so many people that took the journey with me to bring this book to life and I would like to say a deep heartfelt thank you to.

Kelly Hender has had the mammoth task of writing this entire book for me; she's understood my dyslexia better than me, written and rewritten countless times, not to mention she's often had first-hand experience with emotional upheavals in order to write about them! She's become a dear friend in the process and there is no way it would exist without her. Bronwyn Clark is one of the most gentle and patient people I know. She's been involved from the very beginning, taking notes and researching, all the while laughing at my bad jokes. Alexandra Skolarikis is the most organised person I know and is amazing at getting things done. She has been instrumental in research for this book. Angie Menendez has taught me so much about a variety of healing practices through her painstaking research. Nicholas Koutsoukis is such a beautiful man, who has always been happy to research whatever we needed and been the strongest supporter of this work. The very talented Aaron Cliff designed my cover and happily made my million changes—thank you so much! I couldn't have done it without these six people—I thank you so much, more than I can express, for helping me bring this vision to life.

My husband Sam, from the moment I met him has always been a grounding influence in my life. He's also a great supporter of my work and has dutifully read every version of this book. I love you Sam. My beautiful boys, Stephen and Peter, have taught me unconditional love—watching them react to the world around them as they grew has informed my work. They are also very good at making me laugh and giving me strength. I'd like to thank my friends and family; my wonderful parents and siblings, especially my nieces and nephews, for always showing me so much love and support. Also, I'd like to give a special mention to those who supported me in life and who have now passed: Nick Kastellorios, Tess Kastanas and Bella Noble.

So much of what I've learned about healing for this book has been thanks to my clients, who visit me every day and put their faith in the work. The lessons I have seen people go through is astounding and I'm humbled that many of them have returned over many visits and done the hard work to transform their lives.

Kingsford Family Medical Centre has been my home away from home; all the staff, including the doctors and administration staff have been a great support to me.

I'd like also to send a special thanks to Larissa Thrupp and Stacey Petrakis for your input in the beginnings of this book. Also, my wonderful friend Zoe Argiropoulos who has always been there through thick and thin to give me support and strength—thank you so much.

And thank you, reader, for having the courage to buy this book and do the work. I'd love to hear about your journey, drop me a line and tell me your story.

About the author

Leanne Magoulias is a medium, messenger and healer. She communicates with those who have crossed over for the purposes of healing ancestral inherited emotions. Leanne first embarked on her own healing journey more than 25 years ago and uses these insights to help heal her clients. She has assisted the personal growth of thousands of people all over Australia and the rest of the world to find their true purpose.

Leanne is available for phone consultations for clients outside of Sydney who would like assistance with emotional issues such as anxiety, depression, phobias, relationship breakdowns, parenting issues, past-life regression, corporate counselling and reiki.

Look for Leanne's posts on:
Instagram: *instagram.com/leannemagoulias*
Facebook page: *facebook.com/leannemagoulias*
Bookings: *leannemagoulias.com.au*

www.ingramcontent.com/pod-product-compliance
Lightning Source LLC
Chambersburg PA
CBHW062243300426
44110CB00034B/1407